Important issues relating to the promotion of

# Positive Behaviour and Self-Esteem in Secondary Schools

## Jenny Mosley

Positive Press

Published by Positive Press Ltd
28A Gloucester Road
Trowbridge
Wiltshire
BA14 0AA
England


Originally published in card covers and tape binding 1998
Revised and republished in new cover 2002


© Jenny Mosley 1998, 2002


ISBN 0 9530122 8 X

Printed in England

# Acknowledgements

I would like to thank all the secondary schools who have participated in our training and continue to persevere with all the Quality Circle Time initiatives. The 'movement' is growing in the secondary sector; key people from secondary schools are now attending accredited Train the Trainers courses – contact details in the resources section. We are hoping a comprehensive book outlining all current secondary initiatives will evolve from this course.

Meanwhile, I would like to thank Marilyn Tew for her sterling work whilst a consultant with our team – she also helped revamp this book at an earlier stage and we wish her well with her current doctorate. I would also like to thank, in particular, the two headteachers who have contributed the following quotes as they have invested a lot of their time and energy into this model.

*"The Maplesden Noakes School identified the Jenny Mosley Consultancy's Whole School Quality Circle Time, as an exciting model to play a major role in delivering vision of a whole school policy for self-esteem".*

**Douglas Kimber – Headteacher, Maplesden Noakes School, Maidstone**

*"I was moved by what happened – how the circle got to the point where they could express freely their appreciation. I was also struck by the way the group learned so rapidly how to 'do' circle time and how many children progressed even in that short time in terms of their abilities, confidence and self-esteem".*

**Libby Lee – Headteacher, Ralph Allen Secondary School, Bath**

We also wish to thank:

David Fulton Publishers for allowing us to reproduce as a cover illustration the drawing by Meg Mosley, which first appeared on page x of *Quality Circle Time in the Secondary School* by Jenny Mosley and Marilyn Tew.

Ian Gyllenspetz for his lovely cartoon on page 34.

# INTRODUCTION

This booklet has been written to introduce those involved in secondary education to Jenny Mosley's Whole School Quality Circle Time Model. The implementation of the Model leads to:

- ♦ **positive relationships throughout school**
- ♦ **personal, moral and social development in all pupils**
- ♦ **sound self-esteem in all members of the school community**
- ♦ **respectful, democratic school systems**
- ♦ **reduction in bullying**
- ♦ **positive behaviour management**
- ♦ **democratic listening systems which develop a sense of citizenship.**

# THE WHOLE SCHOOL
# QUALITY CIRCLE TIME MODEL

## This model has recommendations, policies and strategies to promote a positive ethos throughout the school day

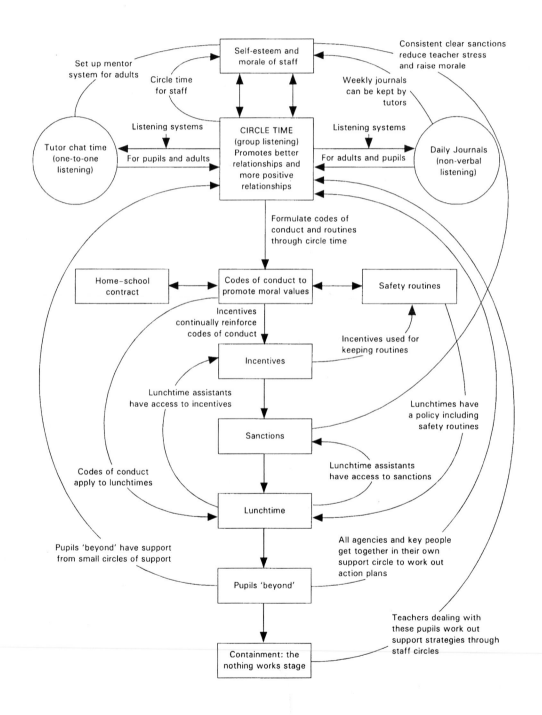

# The need for a coherent approach to enhancing self-esteem and positive relationships

There is an ever-increasing concern from government about standards of achievement in education. League tables and percentage targets for literacy are the spurs used to provoke greater attainment at all levels. Yet, through the years, research has shown behaviour, motivation and learning to be linked to self-perception, personal growth and development. (Lawrence 1988; Maslow, 1962; Rogers 1983, Burns 1982, Greenhalgh 1994.)

Chris Woodhead (quoted by Young in *Times Educational Supplement* 1997) berated pastoral care in schools as:

> *'too often sloppy and sentimental, with teachers wrongly acting as agony aunts'*

and asserted that:

> *'teachers should not be devoting their time to solving pupils' personal problems, or using them as an excuse for poor performance.'*

Yet, as Marianne Talbot (*TES* 1997) points out:

> *'there are many young people whose spiritual and moral existence is promoted only by their school.'*

Schools must involve themselves, then, in promoting pupils' spiritual, moral and social development and this cannot be achieved by concentrating on academic achievement and leaving the explicit promotion of PSE to parents, the church and the community.

# Implications of self-concept development in schools

Coopersmith (1967) cited in Burns (1979, p.294), highlighted three conditions which facilitate high self-esteem in the classroom setting:

1. The teacher's acceptance of the child, while at the same time recognising the child's strengths, problems and limitations. By accepting the child the teacher indicates that the child is worthy of the teacher's attention and respect. This respect enables the child to come to terms with his abilities and limitations.

2. The existence of explicit limits, clearly defined and consistently enforced, which provide standards of conduct and behavioural expectations.

3. The provision of respectful treatment, which is given to pupils who observe limits and act in accordance with rules and guidelines of the classroom.

# A pictorial overview of the self-concept

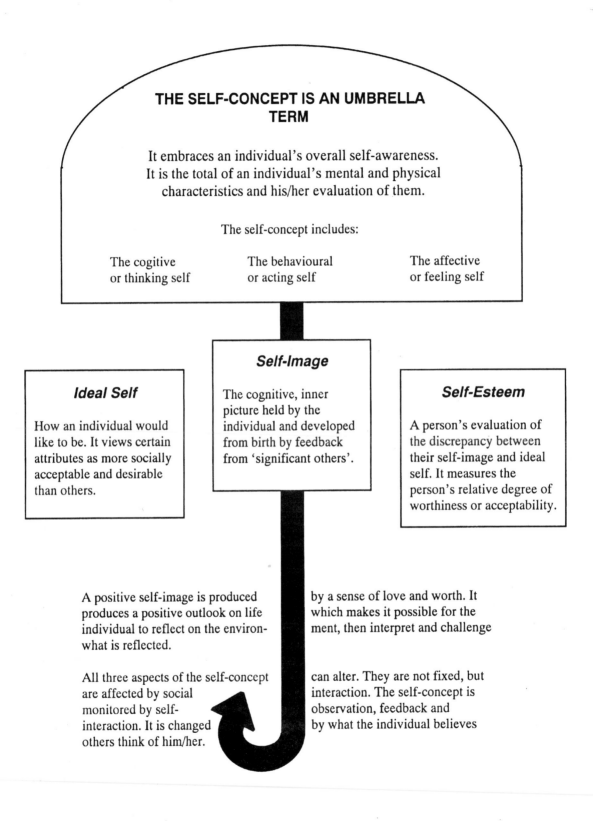

**THE SELF-CONCEPT IS AN UMBRELLA TERM**

It embraces an individual's overall self-awareness.
It is the total of an individual's mental and physical
characteristics and his/her evaluation of them.

The self-concept includes:

| The cogitive or thinking self | The behavioural or acting self | The affective or feeling self |

### Ideal Self

How an individual would like to be. It views certain attributes as more socially acceptable and desirable than others.

### Self-Image

The cognitive, inner picture held by the individual and developed from birth by feedback from 'significant others'.

### Self-Esteem

A person's evaluation of the discrepancy between their self-image and ideal self. It measures the person's relative degree of worthiness or acceptability.

A positive self-image is produced
produces a positive outlook on life
individual to reflect on the environ-
what is reflected.

All three aspects of the self-concept
are affected by social
monitored by self-
interaction. It is changed
others think of him/her.

by a sense of love and worth. It
which makes it possible for the
ment, then interpret and challenge

can alter. They are not fixed, but
interaction. The self-concept is
observation, feedback and
by what the individual believes

Diagram by Marilyn Tew adapted from William James

## Self-concept and behaviour

Burns (1979, p.219) summarises the behaviours that are displayed by people with either unhealthy or healthy self-esteem.

**Those suffering from low or unhealthy self-esteem and lack of worth often display the following characteristic behaviours:**

♦ *They can be very sensitive to criticism, because it is read as giving validity to their inferiority.*

♦ *They can be hypercritical of others in order to defend the shaky self-image and redirect attention on to the shortcomings of others. Personal failure and weakness are denied and any accusation is seen as 'getting at them' or 'somebody else's fault.'*

♦ *They can over respond to flattery because any form of praise is better than no praise.*

♦ *The person with negative feelings of worth is likely to be timid and lack interest in competition.*

**Those with a healthy, positive self-image display the following behaviours:**

♦ *They have an ability to modify strongly-held values and principles in the light of new experience.*

♦ *They show a lack of worry over the past and the future.*

♦ *They have confidence to cope with problems even in the face of the occasional failure.*

♦ *They accept their self as a person of equal worth with others despite differences in specific talents and attributes.*

♦ *They are sensitive to the needs of others.*

It follows that any change in the self-concept towards a greater sense of worth, or higher self-esteem, would alter behaviour. The individual would revise his concept of himself in relation to the world in which he lives and change his behaviour to conform more closely to the expectations of society.

## Self-concept and acceptance of other people

One method of protecting an inadequate self-concept and maintaining psychological security is to put social distance between self and others by creating an out-group. There is powerful identification with the in-group by directing hostility and rejection at the members of the out-group.

Research into the relationship between self-attitude and acceptance of others has demonstrated positive correlations. Some of the 'others' to whom attitudes have been assessed belong to out-groups and ethnic minorities, making it apparent that self-attitudes are positively related to ethnic attitudes and to degrees of tolerance and prejudice. Those with positive feelings about themselves seem to feel free to divorce themselves from stereotyped convention, and appear able to accept and have more positive attitudes towards others.

In summary, the self-accepting person seems to accept other people more readily, sees the world as a more congenial place than the self-rejecter and is less defensive towards others and about him/herself.

## Self-concept and learning

Numerous research studies, summarised by Purkey (1970) and LaBenne and Green (1969) are more than adequate testimony to the fact that low self-esteem tends to produce under-achievement and poor performance levels, and in some cases withdrawal from academic activities. Equally certain is that children who possess positive self-concepts are able to make more positive and clearer appraisals of their ability to perform at school, and produce results that are superior to those of pupils with more uncertain and negative feelings about themselves.

Purkey (1970, p.15) concluded that:

> *'overall the research evidence clearly shows a persistent and significant relationship between the self concept and academic achievement.'*

Lawrence used several counselling approaches with retarded readers and demonstrated a significant gain in reading attainment over control groups. It would seem that modification to self-perception has considerable effects on academic performance. It would appear, however, that the relationship between self-concept and academic attainment is reciprocal, not unidirectional. Academic success raises or maintains self-esteem, while self-esteem influences performance through expectations, standards, recognition of personal strengths, higher motivation and level of persistence.

More recent work (e.g. Gardner 1991, 1993), has taken a wider view of the whole concept of intelligence and an 'intelligent person'. Social intelligence is distinct from academic learning and is a key part of what makes people do well in the practicalities of life. People have a mixture of intellect and emotional acuity, both need developing in order to make productive, mentally healthy, capable adults.

# CIRCLE
# TIME

# WHAT IS CIRCLE TIME?

Circle time is a democratic and creative approach used to consider a wide range of issues affecting the whole school community: teaching staff, pupils, support staff, parents and governors.

Industry calls this method Quality Circle and has been using it since the 1960s to overcome the gulf that can develop between the management and the shop floor, i.e. the 'them and us' attitude. The reputation for quality that Japan enjoys today stems largely from its use of quality circles.

> 'Typically a circle meets once a week for one hour to consider quality problems. Mostly they will tackle problems at the 'earthy' end of the scale ... They will make suggestions for solving them.'
>
> Jim Govan (Institute of Quality Assurance)

## Quality Circle Time in secondary schools

The Whole School Quality Circle Time Model developed by Jenny Mosley is summarised in diagrammatic form on page 2. Quality Circle Time is a group process. It involves a whole class, including the teacher, meeting in a circle at least once a week to look at issues relating to personal, social, moral and health education. The circle meeting has five structures (page 13) that encourage the development of positive relationships, self-discipline, self-regulating behaviour management, conflict resolution, assertive communication and democratic group process, alongside the skills of speaking, listening, observing, thinking and concentrating. Of paramount importance to circle time is emotional 'safety', which is produced by clear ground rules and an attitude that values every person's contribution.

Schools have a vital role to play in supporting parents and others in ensuring that young people develop sufficient emotional understanding to:

- ♦ Be stimulated by their academic learning
- ♦ Develop a range of different skills
- ♦ Form and sustain successful relationships
- ♦ Be an active participator in the community

**Quality Circle Time transforms personal, social education into a process of personal, social development in young people**

## Motivation and achievement

A growing body of knowledge arising from the work of Peter Salovey, Howard Gardner and others, reported initially in Daniel Goleman's book *Emotional Intelligence*, points towards the importance of positive self-esteem in the learning process. This work confirms the findings of Burns (1982), which demonstrated that pupils who have taken part in programmes to raise their awareness of emotions and to enhance their self-esteem quite simply achieve higher scores on standardised achievement tests.

The more pupils understand their emotions, the less likely they are to feel disaffected from the learning process. Instead of channelling their emotional difficulties into bullying, conflict and confrontation with school authorities, they will be able to find ways of engaging in a positive way with the opportunities for many different forms of learning being provided within the school. The National Curriculum lays great emphasis on content and, more than ever before, the education system and educators are under pressure to meet national targets. In order to do this, we need to develop an approach that will enable young people to develop emotionally.

The circle time approach, with its structures and activities, enhances self-esteem and creates a working atmosphere of co-operation. It provides opportunities to:

♦ Reflect upon emotional experience

♦ Understand the experiences of others

♦ Experience connection to the wider society

♦ Make personal decisions based on these understandings

♦ Bring these understandings to bear on the academic subjects being studied.

## Personal and social development and relationships

The circle process enables young people to experience their own uniqueness and find ways to value the distinctive contributions that others who are different from them can make. Quality Circle Time has the deliberate aim of teaching empathy and tolerance. As pupils take part in the circle games, rounds and discussions, they learn the skill of empathy. Increased empathy increases tolerance of difference whether social, cultural or racial. This has an enormous potential to create a society that celebrates its diversity. The schools cited below in OFSTED reports used Quality Circle Time for PSE.

---

**OFSTED report, Warren Comprehensive**

*'The excellent quality of the relationships within the school is evidence that pupils feel respected and valued. This enables them to reflect positively on their experience of life. Circle time, an exercise to raise self-esteem, is used by form tutors.'*

---

**OFSTED report, Northgate Middle School**

*'The school provides many opportunities for moral development. Issues are openly discussed as part of the curriculum and in circle times. Moral values are promoted by teachers through their relationships with pupils and during lessons. In discussions older pupils show good understanding of the issues facing individuals and discuss sensitively issues such as racism and bereavement.'*

## Behaviour and self-discipline

The circle encourages pupils to reflect on their behaviour. They offer and receive an array of advice and suggestions as to how they might change unsatisfactory behaviour. They identify personal targets for improvement and support each other in attempts to reach those targets. They recognise the achievements of their peers and praise them accordingly. There is a gradual shift of the onus of responsibility for discipline from the teacher to the young people themselves. They begin to learn and understand the consequences of their behaviour and take responsibility for themselves and others.

> **OFSTED report, Phoenix Secondary and Primary School (Special School)**
>
> *'Pupils are well behaved and courteous and aware that the school has high expectations of them. Pupils respond well to the 'golden rules' which provide clear guidance for purposeful and positive relationships with peers and adults. Clear definitions of inappropriate behaviour and procedures enable pupils to take responsibility for their own actions.*

## School ethos

Recent research indicates that successful schools are characterised by a healthy climate, a strong ethos that respects and nurtures good relationships with clear, safe and secure boundaries. We cannot transmit moral codes through exhortation or cajole young people into becoming good citizens. Instead we need to provide them with a range of different opportunities to explore their feelings about how they should live their lives and how they should engage with other people.

Quality Circle Time helps create a positive ethos by providing:

- ♦ A space for listening and a space for being listened to
- ♦ A time and a place for reviewing and reflecting on what has been learned
- ♦ A shared and developing language for describing one's own and others' emotions
- ♦ A feeling of community and responsibility.

Tutor periods and registration times, provided space can be kept free from administrative detail, offer the chance for circle time meetings, as do PSE lessons taught by specialist teachers. However it is timetabled, space must be made available to address the key skills of communication, negotiation, conflict resolution, co-operation and assertiveness.

## Positive attitudes

The circle fosters positive attitudes and relationships because of the way in which it is structured. The teacher becomes a role model of positive attitudes, using positive language to affirm helpful social and relational skills. Negative language is avoided in circle meetings so pupils learn that there is no risk of being shown up or ridiculed.

It is important to keep a fast pace through the five structures (see page 13), so there is no time for the discussion to become 'bogged down' and little opportunity for boredom and bad behaviour. The circle time script also ensures that pupils can speak for themselves, but cannot 'get at' other members of the group. 'I' statements are encouraged throughout.

## Quality Circle Time becomes an integral part of whole school policies

- ♦ **Behaviour Policy**
- ♦ **Anti-bullying Policy**
- ♦ **Self-esteem Policy**
- ♦ **Positive relationships Policy**
- ♦ **Assertiveness (at the root of drug and sex education)**

# RULES FOR SUCCESSFUL CIRCLE TIME

The circle runs well when the ground rules are clearly established and everyone adheres to them, including the teacher. A good idea is to have one or two initial circle sessions that include enjoyable exercises (e.g. Pirate & Keys/ Hunter & Hunted/ Killer), then work out ground rules with the whole group. If the group doesn't suggest some of the rules – you propose them.

## Teacher tips for successful circles

- ♦ The first thing to remember is always to be positive during a circle time.

- ♦ You are building an atmosphere of trust and sharing. Sarcasm, dominant behaviour and aggression will inhibit honest communication.

- ♦ Good communication takes place only in a climate of emotional 'safety'. Everyone must be safe from:
  - overt criticism
  - mockery from anyone else
  - teacher's control techniques that involve showing pupils up.

## Ground rules

1. Do not interrupt each other. During the opening round, each person can speak only if they are holding the speaking object (choose an appropriate item). This includes the teacher.

2. No put-downs, mockery, or pointed laughter.

3. No person may be named in a negative way. Criticise the behaviour, not the person. For example, Tom may want to say 'I don't like it when Carl won't let me play football at lunchtime'. In accordance with the ground rules he would have to say, 'I don't like it when

other pupils don't let me play football'. The discussion is now about letting people into games, and what it feels like to be left out, not a war between Tom and Carl!

4. If any pupil does not wish to speak, he/she may say 'Pass'. At the end of the round anyone who chose not to speak can be given a second opportunity.

# Discipline during circle time

Many of the usual techniques used by teachers for maintaining discipline are unhelpful to Quality Circle Time. Instead of naming the behaviour that is unacceptable, the teacher must praise the behaviours that are in accordance with good listening, co-operation and concentration. If someone really won't stop behaving in an unacceptable way, a visual warning (similar to the yellow card used in football) is issued. The person is warned that if they continue to behave inappropriately, they will be put out of the circle and excluded from one of the favourite games that are played at the end of circle time.

I asked a number of teachers who have been involved in using circle time in a variety of contexts to give their opinion of its value.

*'I began using circle time in registration with year 7 groups. I ran six 20-minute sessions and included themes of friendship, co-operation, the community, feelings and self-awareness. Even in these short sessions the tutors and myself have noticed an increase in self-confidence of some students ... It is intended that tutors will continue to use circle time with their tutor groups throughout their school lives, thus providing them with a forum for problem-solving and building self-confidence.'*

C. Atherton, Cranford Community School

*'I think the process itself is extremely valuable and should be available to all groups, especially year 7 where there is the most problem with adjustment either with friends or to the secondary school out of the different expectations of 26 different feeder schools.'*

*'The relaxed approach made people think a lot more about each other.'*

*'I think the circle increased the number of friendships and relationships in the group. They had opportunities to discover more about one another and more in-depth things than in normal discussion. They also sat next to different people all the time because of the way in which the circle worked. The games mixed them up [and] constantly changed the pairs for paired work. They did not have a chance to get into friendship groups and stay there as they do in lessons sat at desks. I think that really helped them to find new people and get to know them.'*

(The Ridgeway School)

# QUALITY CIRCLE TIME STRUCTURE

## Opening game

Pulls the group together, provides sense of fun and enjoyment, used to teach learning skills, moral values and codes of conduct.

## Round

Gives everybody a chance to speak. A speaking object such as a conch can be used. A scripted sentence stem is useful, such as 'I find it easiest to work in class when ...'

## Open forum

Open, free discussion following the round – can be used for problem-solving and target-setting, e.g. 'Is there anyone who wants some help with their behaviour?' Make sure pupils raise their hands before speaking, speak one at a time and listen to each other.

*Script for problem-solving during open forum:*
*Pupils say 'I need help because I ...'*
*('Would it help if I ...?')*
*('Would it help if you ...?')*
*Summary and target setting*

## Celebration of successes

Not necessarily related to theme – just 'thank you' for kind acts during the past week or for praiseworthy attributes, can be pupil to pupil, pupil to adult, adult to pupil.

## Closing game

Brings a sense of closure and bridges into the next part of the school day.

# Some 'starter' ideas for circle time

Remind pupils to use their skills of thinking, looking, listening, speaking and concentrating.

## 1. Examples of rounds

I get fed up when ...
l am afraid of ...
I feel happy when ...
Something I have learned today is ...
I was pleased with myself because ...
I was kind when ...
I like it when ...
I don't like it when ...(*Can lead to* 'Does anyone need some help with their behaviour?')

## 2. Game: The Pirate's Treasure

The 'pirate' sits on a chair in the centre of the circle and is blindfolded. The treasure, e.g. a bunch of keys, is placed under the chair. Obstacles – upturned chairs, school bags, scrunched-up newspaper – are placed around the pirate's chair. A treasure-seeker is selected to negotiate the obstacles and creep up on the pirate to try to capture the treasure. If the pirate hears and successfully points to the treasure-seeker, saying 'stop', the seeker returns to his/her seat and another is chosen. When the treasure is captured, a new pirate is selected. This activity can lead on to discussing 'setting targets in life' and what obstacles can prevent their achievement.

## 3. Game: Silent Circle

A noisy object e.g. tambourine, is passed around the circle trying to avoid any sound being made. This can lead on to 'I like silence because ...'

## 4. Game: Acting Headteachers ('mantle of the expert' – a drama strategy)

The pupils are told they are headteachers of brilliant schools. A few props would be useful, e.g. glasses, briefcase, folder. The teacher uses a 'microphone' to announce: 'We have brought you here today because the BBC has learnt that you have wonderful ideas on how to make children and teachers happy in your schools.' The pupils are invited to take turns in describing the ideas they have implemented in their schools to make life happy and enjoyable. This can lead on to discussion of strategies for making life enjoyable for everyone in school, e.g. rules, codes of conduct, behaviour targets.

# Self-evaluation sheet for teachers starting circle time

|  | Yes | No |
|---|---|---|
| Did I inform the pupils that circle time would be happening? |  |  |
| When the listening systems were set up, did I inform the pupils that, whilst I respect their privacy and right to confidentiality, anything they told me of a particularly worrying nature might have to be taken further? |  |  |
| Did I take a deep breath and create a positive focus before starting? |  |  |
| Was the circle session adequately structured? i.e.<br>a) starting game<br>b) round/follow-up activity<br>c) open forum<br>d) celebrate success<br>e) ending activity |  |  |
| Did I keep to my basic circle time rules? |  |  |
| Did I encourage the pupils to keep their circle time rules i.e. by:<br>a) giving specific praise to pupils practising the social skills<br>b) allowing time for pupils to praise each other<br>c) mentioning how the moral rules incorporate into the activities. |  |  |
| Did I follow an arranged sanction system using a visual warning card followed by time out of the circle? |  |  |
| Did I organise facilities with another teacher whereby any pupil failing to heed warnings and time out could be removed to another classroom with pre-arranged work? |  |  |
| Was the focus of my circle time appropriate for my class? |  |  |
| Was an opportunity provided during open forum for pupils to nominate themselves for help with their behaviour? |  |  |
| Did I encourage the shy pupils to participate? |  |  |
| Were the children given the right to 'pass' in a round and then re-offered the opportunity to speak? |  |  |
| Have I evaluated the circle time with the pupils? |  |  |
| Am I clear how I will follow up any matters arising from circle time? |  |  |

# Continuing success - some pointers

When personal and controversial issues are under discussion warn students only to say as much as they feel is 'safe', i.e. be very sure, from the beginning, to tell them that they are in charge of the information they entrust to the whole group. They must realise that although confidentiality is encouraged it is not guaranteed. Therefore, if there is anything too personal or private which they feel they need to discuss further, suggest to them that they ask to see you for a private chat at a different time.

◆ Perhaps offer to be available one break-time a week.

◆ Don't overdo circle work; making it over long will kill interest.

◆ Make sure you vary the circle approach. It includes warm-ups, games, paired talking/listening exercises, rounds, discussion and role-play.

◆ Evaluate regularly (e.g. 'The most boring/interesting part of this group for me was ...')

◆ Make sure you follow-up any injustices or things that are 'going wrong' for students. Circle work must not exist in isolation. They will learn to trust you only if they perceive you as genuinely caring about their needs and being prepared to do something on their behalf.

◆ Make sure you always take a few minutes to evaluate the session too. If possible set up some form of support with colleagues to discuss the issues that are raised.

◆ Although you obviously will take a serious approach to this sort of work, try to make sure that you include some fun and try to end on a light-hearted note with a closing 'fun' exercise.

# HOW QUALITY CIRCLE TIME ENHANCES SELF-ESTEEM AND POSITIVE BEHAVIOUR

The very act of the whole group being seated in a circle emphasises unity and equality. The fact that everyone can see each other encourages more open and trusting relationships. The structures used within circle sessions also encourage all participants to co-operate, to express their views and to listen to others. They therefore begin to feel more valued and worthwhile members of that group.

The issues and problems that are highlighted in circle sessions emerge from the participants themselves. They are, therefore, the most important focus. The framework of sitting within a circle, taking a turn to speak and joining in all the activities, convey important messages regarding authority and control to all the participants. The leader's role is facilitative, encouraging pupils to feel that they too, have the authority and self-control to attempt to solve the behaviour, learning and relationship problems that concern them. By contributing to this problem-solving process, individuals are motivated to take more self and collective responsibility.

People involved in circle programmes feel a part of a group they can trust; (ground rules for circle sessions are devised by the whole group to help build this feeling of 'safety'.) Within the circle approach, feelings and views are being acknowledged and acted upon, so participants are able to reorganise their self-perceptions in a more positive way and thus acquire a sounder self-concept. Moreover, the structures and techniques used within circle time teach people how to become more clear, direct and honest with each other. Individuals are given time both to volunteer their own concerns for group help and to offer help and encouragement to others. By learning to express their feelings in a calm way they are learning to develop assertive relationships and therefore are learning that they don't have to resort to aggressive, manipulative or withdrawn behaviour in order to have their needs recognised.

Quality Circle Time ensures that all people feel valued as all personal and social achievements are acknowledged and celebrated by the staff and class group.

## Maslow and circle time

Maslow (1962) proposed a hierarchy of human need. His view was that in order for people to function at the top of the hierarchy, their needs must be met at the lower levels. The most basic human needs are to have enough to eat and drink, to be neither too hot nor too cold. Once those needs are satisfied, a person needs a sense of emotional safety. If there is constant uncertainty or danger, attention and energy are used for protection, rather than for any higher learning functions. Emotional safety gives the foundation for love, affection and belonging, which according to Maslow, are basic human drives. Only when the people feel that they belong in some social context do they begin to build self-esteem and approach new learning situations with confidence.

The diagram shows how Maslow's hierarchy of needs fits with group work and circle time.

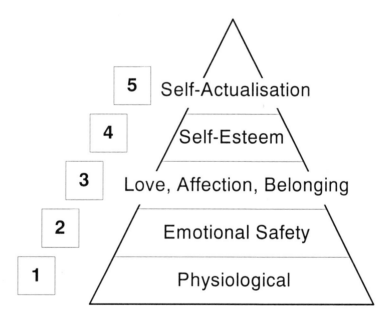

### Applying Maslow's model of needs to the benefits of group work

Stage 1: Sitting in a circle allows everyone to see each other and to 'pick up' signs of physical distress very quickly, e.g. if people are too tired.

Stage 2: Ground rules help people create emotional safety within group. Trust builds as people adhere to these over a period of time.

Stage 3: Group work promotes a feeling of belonging which generates affection and care for other members.

Stage 4: Being part of a group, having significance and value within that group, enhances peoples' self-esteem. The group can help people set small realistic targets and then celebrate their success.

Stage 5: Group work provides people with opportunities to try out ideas and encourages them to realise their creative potential within a safe setting. This positive experience can then give them the strength to try out a similar creative approach in their daily life.

# HOW QUALITY CIRCLE TIME MEETINGS CAN HELP A SCHOOL

**Regular circle time can help to:**

⇨ **Build friendships**

⇨ **Create trust**

⇨ **Eliminate put-downs**

⇨ **Promote personal and collective responsibility**

⇨ **Encourage self-discipline**

⇨ **Improve listening skills**

⇨ **Promote better behaviour**

⇨ **Develop personal integrity**

⇨ **Develop empathy**

⇨ **Create a sense of belonging**

⇨ **Teach assertive skills**

⇨ **Solve problems**

⇨ **Promote understanding**

⇨ **Improve relationships**

⇨ **Integrate all special needs children with the whole class**

# Some Implications Arising from a Small-scale Study of a Circle-based Programme Initiated for the Tutorial Period

JENNY MOSLEY, *John of Gaunt Comprehensive School, Trowbridge*

Some tutors and their pupils are reluctant to participate in active groupwork strategies. Jenny Mosley reports upon a circle-based programme of activities within the ordinary tutorial period which she initiated. Her evaluation reveals that all participants recognised the practical benefits to be gained from a circle approach to active learning, and provides useful examples of the techniques she used.

## Introduction

This article arose from pupil and teacher observations of a five week 'intervention' programme, initiated by myself for 25 second year pupils and their form tutor, during their weekly half-hour tutorial period.

Underpinning any teaching enterprise are implicit, often unacknowledged, beliefs about the nature of knowledge, of children and learning. These inform a view of what teaching is or should be: embedded in this is a diversity of meanings attached to such con-cepts as authority and control. It is essential then, that I should attempt to make explicit my own position in relation to these theoretical considerations in order to clarify the rationale for initiating the programme; only then is it possible to assess its effectiveness.

## Rationale for Programme

'... In most conceptions [of education], knowledge is assumed to be objective; a body of principles, laws and theories, etc. external to the learner ...'

(Taylor and Richards 1985)

Opposed to this is a view which insists on the importance of *personal* knowledge or as Salmon (1980) phrases it: 'people as knowers'.

Knowledge in this context is seen as a process able to extend the learner's experience through their personal involvement with the subject matter. Indeed, currently there are relevant centrally sponsored initiatives such as Profiling, CPVE, TVEI and GCSE which do give fresh emphasis to pupil experience and attempt to focus on what a pupil *can* do rather than cannot do and which hold within them the potential for transforming the character of secondary schooling. The critical task for the teacher, alert to this possibility, is to ensure that 'experience' is then reflected and 'worked upon' so that it may lead to knowledge. As a result knowledge may be given back its necessary personal dimension. Even so it must be remembered that education is a social process which requires that we must work together to understand each other's world. I am indebted to those writers and researchers who emphasise the personal nature of know-ledge and concur with Salmon (1980) that current theories of learning have little to offer precisely because they deny the individual's unique personal contexts.

The social interaction process is vital for mediating knowledge. As learning is rooted in interpersonal relationships, it is crucial that the teacher, concerned to foster meaningful learning, should seriously enquire into its necessary enabling attitudes and conditions. A decision as to what these may be, is obviously governed not only by the previous concerns but is also influenced by a particular view of the child.

*[The article continues, see Journal as referenced above.]*

Salmon, P. (ed.) (1980) Coming to know. London: Routledge & Kegan Paul
Taylor, P. & Richards, R. (1985) Curriculum Studies. NFER: Nelson.

# CIRCLE TIME AND THE ELTON REPORT

## Key recommendations of the Report[1]

R18   Headteachers should ensure, by consistent policy-making and encouragement, that all teachers accept responsibility for maintaining good behaviour throughout the school and that they model the types of behaviour encouraged by school policy.

R19   Headteachers should promote the development of both management support and peer support within the staff team, and the professional development of its members.

R21   Headteachers and teachers should, in consultation with governors, develop whole school behaviour policies, which are clearly understood by pupils, parents and other school staff.

R23   Schools should strike a healthy balance between rewards and punishments. Both should be clearly specified.

R25   Headteachers and teachers should ensure that rules are applied consistently by all members of staff, but that there is flexibility in the use of punishments to take account of individual circumstances.

R30   All parties involved in the planning, delivery and evaluation of the curriculum should recognise that the quality of its content and the teaching and learning methods through which it is delivered are important influences on pupil behaviour.

R32   Schools should not use rigid streaming arrangements to group their pupils by ability. They should take full account of the implications for pupil behaviour when reviewing their arrangements for grouping pupils. Schools should:

R33.1 Distribute their teaching and other resources equitably across the ability range.

R33.2 Provide a range of rewards accessible to pupils of all abilities.

R38   Secondary headteachers and teachers should identify clear aims for the use of tutorial time. These aims should include reinforcing the school's behaviour policy.

R39.1 Headteachers and teachers should recognise the importance of ascertaining pupils' views.

R43   LEAs should provide in-service training in basic counselling skills for senior pastoral staff at least.

R52.2 Headteachers and teachers, when moving about the school, should be aware of and take responsibility for pupils' behaviour.

R54   LEAs and governing bodies that employ school staff should ensure that midday supervisors are given adequate training in the management of pupil behaviour.

R.57  Headteachers and teachers should ensure that parents receive positive and constructive comments on their children's work and behaviour as a matter of course.

R60.1 Headteachers and teachers should develop an active partnership with parents as an aid to promoting good behaviour.

---

[1] *Discipline in Schools: Report of the Committee of Enquiry.* London, HMSO 1989

R75    Headteachers and teachers should give pupils every opportunity to take responsibilities and to make a full contribution to improving behaviour in schools.

R89    Teachers should take account of gender differences involved in pupils' behaviour, for example by not reinforcing attention-seeking and aggressive behaviour.

R91    Teachers should recognise the potential for injustice and the practical dangers of stereotyping certain kinds of pupils as troublemakers.

R92    Teachers should guard against misinterpreting non-verbal signals and speech patterns of pupils from different cultural backgrounds.

R93    Teachers should avoid modelling any kind of insulting or discriminating behaviour.


**Lord Elton wrote in the foreword to Jenny Mosley's book *Turn Your School Round*:**

> **'This book embodies some of the most important principles established by the Committee of Enquiry into Discipline in Schools set up in 1988 under my chairmanship ... A central group of those recommendations urged every school to develop a 'whole school behaviour policy' involving, and supported by, everyone directly involved with the school itself ... It has been very encouraging to hear, from many witnesses, of the success of her work in improving good schools and 'turning round' those in difficulty, as it endorses some of the Committee's most important findings.'**

# Some important findings of the Report

*Quality Circle Time can play a crucial part in implementing the following findings, quoted from the Elton Report:*

## 1. Classroom management

Our survey shows that teachers see talking out of turn and other forms of persistent, low-level disruption as the most frequent and wearing kind of classroom misbehaviour. Low-level disruption is not a new feature of classroom life. All of us remember from our own school days that some teachers had problems with their classes and others did not. Those who did not were by no means always older or stricter. They were teachers we respected and very often liked. Such teachers knew how to get the best out of groups of children.

Our evidence shows a very broad measure of agreement across the education service (headteachers' and teachers' professional associations, training establishments, LEAs and individual teachers) that a teacher's general competence has a strong influence on his or her pupils' behaviour. There is also a broad measure of agreement on what a teacher needs to be fully effective. Knowledge of the subject to be taught is obviously crucial. So is the ability to plan and deliver a lesson, which flows smoothly and holds pupils' attention. The third area of competence comprises a range of skills associated with managing groups of pupils. It includes the ability to relate to young people, to encourage them in good behaviour and learning, and to deal calmly but firmly with inappropriate or disruptive behaviour. As a useful shorthand we refer to it in our report as 'group management skills'.

Our evidence suggests that the importance of group management skills tends to be underestimated by teachers and by their trainers. This was confirmed by our expert witnesses. We find this worrying because it is the area of competence which relates most directly to pupil behaviour.

Teachers with good group management skills are able to establish positive relationships with their classes based on mutual respect. They can create a classroom climate in which pupils lose rather than gain popularity with their classmates by causing trouble. They can also spot a disruptive incident in the making, choose an appropriate tactic to deal with it and nip it in the bud. They always seem to know what is going on behind their backs. Good group managers understand how groups of young people react to each other and to teachers. They also understand and are in full control of their own behaviour. They model the good behaviour they expect of pupils. All this requires an impressive range of professional skills.

We appreciate the difficulty of the task facing teachers, and the fact that most of them tackle it well every day. This deserves recognition and respect. We also recognise that teachers need support from a variety of sources. Many of our recommendations aim to provide or improve their support. We do not underestimate the seriousness of classroom violence. It is rare but it happens. Teachers who are attacked should have the strongest possible backing and we make recommendations to this effect in Chapter 10.

Our evidence suggests however that there are teachers who lack confidence in their own ability to deal with disruption and who see their classes as potentially hostile. They create a negative classroom atmosphere by frequent criticism and rare praise. They make use of loud public reprimands and threats. They are sometimes sarcastic. They tend to react aggressively to minor incidents. Their methods increase the danger of a major confrontation not only with individual pupils but with the whole class.

Young people rightly see this kind of defensive style as a sign of weakness. Like anyone else they react badly to frequent criticism, sarcasm and aggression. A class will feel no goodwill towards teachers who behave in this way. Their punishments will be seen as unjust and vindictive. In this atmosphere pupils will gain status with their classmates by challenging the teacher's authority.

Serious classroom disruption usually comes about by a process of escalation. It is very unusual for serious trouble to start without a build-up. Escalation from minor incidents can have serious results, such as teachers being verbally abused by pupils. Several of our expert witnesses emphasised the importance of understanding escalation and avoiding it by appropriate intervention.

Teachers suffer from quite high levels of occupational stress, and we would expect difficulties with pupils' behaviour to contribute to these. Research evidence ... confirms our impressions. Most teachers work in situations where they are the only adult in a room full of children. If relationships are good the experience can be very rewarding. If not it can be very stressful. Teachers who lack group management skills will experience that feeling and the resulting stress will make them even less effective. Growing anxiety will also make their relationships with pupils more difficult and increase their tendency to overreact to minor incidents.

A few letters we received came close to saying that group management should not be part of a teacher's job. We reject this view. Teaching has never just been about the transmission of knowledge and never will be. Establishing good relationships with pupils, encouraging them to learn and to behave well have always been essential parts of a teacher's work. This cannot be achieved by talking at children, but by working with them.

## 2. Training in group management skills

A more common belief is that group management skills are simply a natural gift. You either have it or you don't. Our evidence does not support this belief. Its most damaging feature is that teachers who have difficulty controlling classes tend to put this down to personal inadequacy rather than to a lack of particular skills which can be acquired through training or advice from colleagues.

The most talented 'natural' teachers may need little training or advice because they learn so quickly from experience. At the other extreme, there are a few teachers for whom training and advice will not be properly effective because their personalities do not match the needs of the job. It is clear, however, that the majority of teachers can become more effective classroom managers as a result of the right kinds of training, experience and support.

Teachers have tended to stay out of each others' classrooms and not to talk about their own discipline problems. Too often teachers do not seek help because it feels like an admission of incompetence, and they do not offer it because it feels like accusing a colleague of incompetence. As a result the tradition of classroom isolation persists in many schools.

The beliefs that either group management skills should not be necessary or that they cannot be learned seem to be traditional in parts of the profession. Our evidence suggests that these beliefs contribute significantly towards teacher stress. This is further increased by the more widespread tradition of classroom isolation. We see these beliefs or traditions as barriers to good teaching. They should be removed as quickly as possible.

We have described how teachers' traditional reluctance to talk about discipline problems or to let colleagues into their classrooms feeds into a spiral of less effective group management and mounting stress. Support from colleagues as professional equals, which we call 'peer support', is a way of breaking out of that spiral. The peer support group is a valuable resource which is as yet little used in British schools. We were impressed by accounts of its effectiveness in the Australian state of Victoria and by our observation of a similar group in action in a school in North Tyneside. A peer support group is led by a 'facilitator' who is responsible for convening the group and chairing its discussions. It meets regularly on a voluntary basis to talk about classroom management skills. The group can work on three levels. First, its discussions are a very effective form of in-service training. We were given evidence that teachers often learn more about classroom skills by talking to each other than by listening to visiting 'experts'. A peer support group provides regular opportunities for sharing experiences and skills. Second, it helps to break down the tradition of isolation by opening the classroom door. Peer support groups can develop the kind of trust and confidence which lead to mutual observation and consultation, which involves watching and commenting on each other's teaching. This is probably the most effective method of classroom skills training available. Third, it helps to reduce occupational stress. Knowing that even the most experienced teachers can have classroom management problems and that it is acceptable to admit them is a good way of reducing stress. The feeling that it is possible to do something about those problems is even more reassuring.

Later in this chapter we recommend the promotion of peer support through in-service training. It would spread more quickly if new teachers arrived in schools expecting to find a peer support group. *We therefore recommend that initial teacher training establishments should introduce students to the concept of peer support and its uses.*

## 3. Praise and rewards

Several of our witnesses commented on the lack of praise for good behaviour in many schools and emphasised its importance. Most schools have a range of rewards for good academic work or effort such as good marks, good reports, prizes etc., but they tend to benefit a limited group of children. We are left with the disturbing impression that in some schools a pupil can only get attention in one or other of two ways – by working or by behaving badly.

Rewards for pupils may include such things as commendation, merit marks, and letters home. We believe that they should cover the broadest possible range of academic and non-academic achievements, for example, group projects and community service. Telling parents about their children's achievements, as well as any behaviour problems, should be an important part of this system. *We recommend that schools should stride a healthy balance between rewards and punishments and that both should be clearly specified.*

## 4. Midday supervisors

Our visits convinced us that non-teaching staff and, in particular, midday supervisors play an important part in promoting good behaviour. They need to be recognised as an important part of the school community. The school's behaviour policy needs to be made clear to them. So should the action they can take to support it. Governors should support the policy in principle and in detail. We discuss their role in Chapter 9. Parents have a very important part to play in encouraging their children to behave well in school. We discuss this later in this chapter and in Chapter 5. Where they have not been involved in developing it, the school's behaviour policy, and the principles and reasons behind it, should be communicated to them as clearly as possible.

## 5. Bullying and racial/sexual harassment

Misbehaviour is usually defined as behaviour which causes concern to teachers. But there are also some serious forms of bad behaviour, which only or mainly affect pupils. Bullying and racial harassment are cases in point. Bullying includes both physical and psychological intimidation. Recent studies of bullying in schools suggest that the problem is widespread and tends to be ignored by teachers. In Norway our attention was drawn to the work of Olweus and other Scandinavian researchers which analyses similar problems there. Research suggests that bullying not only causes considerable suffering to individual pupils but also has a damaging effect on school atmosphere. This is perhaps even more true of racial harassment. The Commission for Racial Equality expressed concern to us about accounts of racist name-calling, graffiti and physical attacks in schools. We consider that sexual harassment is also an aspect of bullying, and are concerned that this was given very little attention in the evidence put before us. It is hard to see how a school can win the confidence of its pupils if it fails to deal with behaviour which so seriously damages the quality of their lives.

## 6. Tutorial time

In their recent survey report on secondary schools, HMI comment that there are still too many schools which are not making good use of tutorial time. Tutor periods are usually at the beginning of the school day. A session which just consists of taking the register and killing time before the bell goes gets the day off to a bad start for a number of reasons. First, the opportunity to foster commitment to the school has been lost. Second, the pupil is not taken seriously. Third, there is no crossing of a psychological frontier which helps young people take up the role of pupil, rather than son or daughter, and which demonstrates that adults have taken up the role of teachers rather than parents or childminders. The quality of this opening session of the school day is, we believe, crucial for creating a climate of mutual expectations which lead to purposeful behaviour during the day.

## 7. Pupil feedback

The tutor group system can also provide valuable information from pupils on the problems that they see around the school. Seeing the school from the pupils' point of view is important for heads and teachers. Knowing what pupils see as positive helps them improve the atmosphere. Although they may not realise it, schools that do not use their pastoral systems in this way to provide them with feedback receive it nonetheless through bad behaviour. Primary class teachers are well placed to gather this kind of information from pupils. In larger secondary schools, a more formal system is needed. Form tutors and other pastoral staff should provide channels of communication through which the senior management team and the staff as a whole can pick up the feelings of the pupils about their school. This is a valuable source of management information. Where they exist, school councils on which pupils are represented can also provide a forum for constructive discussion. We consider school councils in Chapter 6. PSE programmes can also provide opportunities for exploring pupils' perceptions of the school. *We recommend that headteachers and teachers should:*
1. *recognise the importance of ascertaining pupils' views*
2. *organise systems for doing so and for taking the information gathered into account in the management of the school.*

## 8. Counselling

Effective schools seem to be able to combine high expectations with a sympathetic atmosphere. Teachers are not social workers or psychotherapists. They cannot solve a pupil's home problems however much they may sympathise with them. Rutter found that schools in which teachers saw misbehaviour as a disciplinary rather than a welfare problem tended to achieve better standards of behaviour. He also found better behaviour in schools where teachers made themselves available to be consulted by children about their problems. These findings are not inconsistent with one another. They illustrate the need to strike this balance. We therefore recommend that headteachers and teachers should ensure that pastoral care in schools is characterised by a healthy balance between challenge and support for pupils.

We are convinced that there are skills, which all teachers need, to be involved in listening to young people and encouraging them to talk about their hopes and concerns before coming to a judgement about their behaviour. We consider that these basic counselling skills are particularly valuable for creating a supportive school atmosphere. The skills needed to work effectively with adults whether teachers or parents, are equally crucial. We therefore recommend that initial teacher training establishments should introduce all their students to basic counselling skills and their value. We regard such skills as particularly important for a senior pastoral staff (deputy heads, heads of house and year).
*We recommend that LEAs should provide in-service training in basic counselling skills for senior pastoral staff at least*

Quoted from: Lord Elton (Chairman), *Discipline in Schools: Report of the Committee of Enquiry.* London, HMSO 1989

# POSITIVE RELATIONSHIPS BASED ON SOUND SELF-ESTEEM

# PROMOTING SELF-ESTEEM AND GOOD RELATIONSHIPS

Research shows that teachers with high self-esteem positively affect the self-esteem of their pupils and have better relationships in their classrooms (Lawrence 1988 and Burns 1982).

Self-esteem is the 'inner picture' that we hold of ourselves and our limitations and strengths. This self-image has been built in response to our experiences with other people in the past. The way we were treated and talked to by our family, our teachers, our friends, work colleagues or even the way 'life' has treated us affected the self-picture, as did the way we responded to different events, illnesses or lack of advantages.

## Good self-esteem

Good self-esteem brings a sense of competence and worth. People with good self-esteem will welcome and enjoy new experiences and be able to relate well to others. They exude confidence and optimism, which brings a positive approach to personal and professional life. They learn from criticism, mistakes and failures. They hold the different aspects of life in perspective and so maintain a sense of balance.

## Low self-esteem

Low self-esteem brings a sense of uselessness and incompetence. Lack of confidence can bring self-doubt, occasional self-pity and difficulty in sustaining meaningful relationships with others. People with low self-esteem protect themselves from hurt by either being aggressive and 'putting other people down' or withdrawing into a lonely 'shell'.

*Building self-esteem is vital for the realisation of true potential*

# Ideas for promoting pupil self-esteem

A group of secondary heads produced the following list of methods that could be used to promote self-esteem among pupils.

1. Merits – earned for different things. Collated – values recorded
2. Ethos – everyone treated with respect including pupil- pupil
3. One-to-one counselling
4. Profiling (Record of Achievements)
5. Children invited with parents on parent evenings
6. Display work
7. Achievements board
8. Newsletter – pupil-centred
9. Portfolios of best work
10. Schools Council – status – power – integrity – formal
11. Pupil responsibility for own learning
12. Published rules – values – explicit
13. Mixed ability – small classes
14. Leading by example
15. Credit system – academic/social performance. Totals up to give financial reward
16. Contracting – seeking ideas from pupils and approval from peers
17. Pupils' representation to governors. Pupils learn constraints imposed on teachers
18. Positive marketing policy
19. Contact with a member of staff other than tutor/subject teacher – deputy head involvement
20. Support groups run by heads of year
21. 'Stilling' exercises –  Diaries of Reflection – Journals between pupil and tutor
22. Prefect system – with responsibilities
23. Support groups for parents in building self-esteem
24. KNOW EVERY PUPIL BY NAME – CLASS TEACHER / FORM TUTOR
25. Clearly achievable steps in curriculum

# DEVELOPING GOOD RELATIONSHIPS

Research (Rogers) has shown that there are three fundamental skills to making effective relationships. These skills can be best described under three headings – **respect**, **genuineness** and **empathy**. They are the same skills as those used in counselling.

## Respect

This is behaviour that can make others feel that they are important, worthwhile and special in some way.

RESPECT can be shown by:
>Giving positive attention
>Active listening
>Giving your time freely without making the person feel intrusive
>Remembering the person's name
>Introducing yourself
>Basic courtesies, e.g. offering a chair, making the person feel comfortable
>Asking questions gently
>Checking out assumptions you have made about the other person
>Not interrupting or talking over the other person.

## Genuineness

Behaviour that conveys to others that you too are human, trustworthy, not hiding behind roles or facades, spontaneous and open about yourself in an appropriate manner, 'coming across as being real – not a phoney'.

GENUINENESS is conveyed by:
>Talking appropriately about yourself
>Responding naturally
>Sharing feelings appropriately
>Being spontaneous and honest
>Verbal behaviour consistent with non-verbal signs
>Not being defensive
>Not pretending to be someone or something you are not.

## Empathy

Behaviour that shows that you understand the other person's world as they are experiencing it. In other words, you 'see it their way'.

EMPATHY is shown by:
>Reflecting back to the other person feelings you are picking up – 'You must have felt very angry', 'You sound very happy'.
>Sharing related experiences of your own
>Showing warmth

# A possible model for the generation of stress in pupils and staff

Stress sabotages good relationships. Stressed people do not have the capacity to listen well.

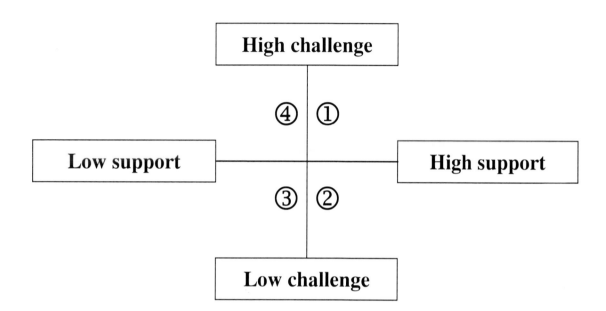

♦ **Where do you fit on this model?**

♦ **How supportive is your school, how much professional challenge do you have?**

♦ **Where do the pupils of your school fit on this model?**

# COMMUNICATION SKILLS

## Counselling

Read again the recommendations of the **Elton Report** where they particularly concern counselling, quoted in full on page 25.

*'We consider that these basic counselling skills are particularly valuable for creating a supportive school atmosphere.'*

---

### A definition of counselling

People become engaged in counselling when a person occupying regularly or temporarily the role of counsellor offers or agrees explicitly to offer time, attention and respect to another person or persons.

The task of the counsellor is to give the other person an opportunity to explore, discover and clarify ways forward that are more resourceful, and help them to a greater sense of wellbeing.

---

When do you need your counselling skills?

Think about all the anxieties and difficult situations staff or pupils might bring to you. Make a list of them and decide which might be helped by you using counselling skills. How did you work this out?

When else should you think about using these counselling skills?

# Helpful and unhelpful ways of responding to people

| Verbal | Non-verbal |
|---|---|
| ☑ uses understandable words | ☑ maintains good eye contact |
| ☑ reflects back and clarifies the person's statements | ☑ occasional head nodding |
| ☑ appropriately interprets | ☑ facial animation |
| ☑ summarises for person | ☑ occasional smiling |
| ☑ responds to primary message | ☑ occasional hand gesturing |
| ☑ use verbal reinforcers, e.g. 'mm-mm', 'Yes', 'I see' | ☑ close physical proximity *if comfortable* |
| ☑ calls person by first name or 'you' | ☑ moderate rate of speech |
| ☑ appropriately gives information | ☑ body shows interest |
| ☑ answers questions about self | ☑ occasional appropriate touching |
| ☑ uses humour occasionally to reduce tension | |
| ☑ is non-judgemental | |
| ☑ adds greater understanding to person's statement | |
| ☑ makes interpretations tentatively so as to elicit genuine feedback from person | |

| Verbal | Non-verbal |
|---|---|
| ☒ advice giving | ☒ looking away from person |
| ☒ preaching | ☒ sitting far apart or turned from person |
| ☒ placating | ☒ frowning |
| ☒ blaming | ☒ tight mouth |
| ☒ cajoling | ☒ distracting gestures |
| ☒ exhorting | ☒ yawning |
| ☒ extensive probing and questioning – especially 'why' questions | ☒ unpleasant tone of voice |
| ☒ directing, demanding | ☒ too slow or too fast rate of speech |
| ☒ patronising attitude | |
| ☒ over-interpretation | |
| ☒ using words person does not understand | |
| ☒ straying from topic | |
| ☒ intellectualising | |
| ☒ over-analysing | |
| ☒ talking about self too much | |

*Our attitudes and the way we handle situations are very important.*

*Through stress and lack of time we get trapped in negative circles*

It is often difficult when we are stressed or annoyed not to criticise a pupil, but it is possible to achieve the effect that we desire in a more positive way.

*'Why do you go on being the same, when I've told you time and again what you are like?'*

## What do we say? Our words are crucial

'Well John! You've made a total mess of it as usual.'

*'You haven't quite understood this section here John. Bring your book out and I'll go through it with you.'*

'What do you think you are doing Matthew?'

*'Matthew, it's time you put that book away and started work on your history project.'*

# Special listening skills

It is of vital importance that a teacher accurately understands what the person is trying to communicate to him/her and in order to do this s/he must use the special listening skills.

## 1. Compassion and warmth

Initially the pupil must be encouraged to feel comfortable with the teacher. This can be achieved by a simple statement or question showing concern, e.g.:

'I'd like to help you ... Can you tell me what's worrying you?'

## 2. Encouragement

Encourage the pupil further, e.g.:

'I know this is very hard for you but you're doing really well.'

## 3. Elucidation

Help the pupil to elaborate and provide all the necessary information, e.g.:

'Are you saying ...?' 'Can you tell me more about ...?'

## 4. Restatement

Check you have understood exactly what the pupil is trying to communicate, e.g.:

'I believe from your statements that you think ...'

## 5. Reflection

Reflect and clarify the information you have received to help the person understand his/her feelings and to show that you have clearly understood what s/he wishes to communicate to you, e.g.:

'You are angry and hurt that ...'

## 6. Summarisation

Summarise the issues raised, e.g.:

'I understand that you are mainly concerned about ...'

# IDEAS FOR ACTIVE TUTORIAL WORK

**For evaluation and closure purposes do a round of:**
What am I taking away with me from this group?
What I'll think of on the way home and wish I had said or done.
The most boring/exciting part of this group for me was ...
Something I have discovered today ...
The homework I am giving myself for next week is ...
My new friend from this group is ...

*Each member of the group takes a card and writes on it something that s/he cares deeply about. This can be written at any length and in any style or form and no topic is forbidden. The member then signs the card and can also write on it whether they want their card to be read out to the group or not. The same applies to their name. After the leader has read the cards to the group, the group can discuss any comments or reactions.*

Procedure: Get a partner, preferably one you don't know. Decide which one is A and which one B. A has three minutes (longer if you like) to tell B about his/her life, starting as far back as possible and continuing in chronological order. B just listens. At the end of three minutes they change round and B talks. At the end of the second three minutes the leader tells them to change partners and decide which is A and B. A carries on from where s/he left off without filling in the missing information and takes three minutes as before. Then it is his new partner's turn. This whole process is repeated three times in this manner and then on the fourth round the leader instructs the partners to talk about their autobiography of the future.

In a circle, each person makes a statement beginning with 'I resent ...' (ordinarily, in relation to the work just completed, or the experience in the class or group).
Repeat the round, beginning with 'I appreciate ...'
Before starting, make sure that everyone understands the meaning of both words. No one is allowed to comment.
Anyone can say 'Pass', which means 'No comment'. Anyone can say: 'I resent nothing', or 'I appreciate nothing'.

*Procedure: Played in a circle. Ask everyone, including the leader, to complete this sentence anonymously on a piece of paper. Put the paper in a container in the centre. Pass round the container, stopping at each person while s/he takes and reads the contribution, enlarging on the sentence and trying to express what the person was feeling. E.g. (Read) 'In this class I am afraid that I will be laughed at ...' (Continue talking) 'I am afraid to say my feelings because everyone laughs at me, so I never say anything.' Continue round the circle. Leader must make sure that everyone just listens, and does not comment. No arguing or comment is allowed. Then discuss what was noticed or discovered.*

Sit in a circle, pass a card to each player, who peeks at it and keeps it hidden. Watch each other. Queen of Spades is the 'Murderer'. If s/he winks at you, you wait a few seconds, throw your card in the centre and say 'I'm dead'. Do not tell who killed you. (Once you are dead, you can say nothing.) If you think you know the 'murderer', say, 'I accuse ...' If you're wrong, you throw your card in: you have committed 'suicide'. Game ends when the 'murderer' is discovered.

Leader says: 'Most of us find it easier to say what is wrong with others and are slightly embarrassed to say what we like about them. Psychologists believe that all this criticism or negative words can lead to a poor image of ourselves and can in extreme cases help to cause mental illness. They believe we all feel much better if we also receive good, positive, accurate messages about ourselves. This is a game where we practise giving positive praise to our neighbour. Each of us will say something we like about our neighbour on the left. It must be honest and it must be something they do or something they can control. I will start the process:'
'The thing I like about (name the person on left) is ...'

a) Brainstorm 'feeling' words.
Leader writes these words on coloured card.

b) Leader holds up a card (e.g. card says 'embarrassed' or 'hateful'). Members complete sentence using word: 'I feel embarrassed when ...'

c) Groups of three, pick words at random, make mime or short play using all the three words (feelings).

d) Relate true experiences. 'The last time I felt really embarrassed was when ...'

e) Speak for someone else, check accuracy. E.g.(Sally is speaking for Joan): I'm Joan and I feel embarrassed when I'm asked to speak out in class. 'Is that true Joan?' Joan answers and discusses Sally's statement.

Which would you prefer to be out of each of these pairs?

| | |
|---|---|
| 1.cat | dog |
| 2. rich | poor |
| 3. rich | beautiful |
| 4. happy | sad |
| 5. horse | sheep |
| 6. bat | ball |
| 7. tree | flower |
| 8. left | right |

# REWARDS AND SANCTIONS CREATE BOUNDARIES AND PROVIDE MOTIVATION

# UNDERPINNING RULES OR CODES OF CONDUCT

No system of rewards or sanctions is meaningful without an agreed set of values, which everyone in the community works towards. So often school rules are a mixture of moral values and institutional routines. Both are extremely important for the smooth running of the school and the safety of the people who work there. Both sets of rules inform behaviour, yet they are different.

## Moral values or codes of conduct

Moral values describe the principles that inform judgements about what is good or bad. People's attitudes (disposition or inclination towards other people and their actions) are largely built on what they value. Both values and attitudes inform behaviour.

The Jenny Mosley Whole School Model proposes that schools agree a set of values that everyone upholds. They are explicitly written in every room and taught through Quality Circle Time activities. These values reflect those that underpin the laws of society and cover respect for

♦ people's bodies
♦ people's feelings
♦ property
♦ time and work

Primary schools using the model write the rules as six statements with a 'do' and a 'don't'.

| | |
|---|---|
| Do listen | Don't interrupt |
| Do work hard | Don't waste your time or other people's |
| Do look after property | Don't waste or damage it |
| Do be gentle | Don't hurt anybody |
| Do be kind | Don't hurt anyone's feelings |
| Do be honest | Don't cover up the truth |

The rewards accompany the 'do' side of the rules. Sanctions accompany the 'don'ts'.

## Routines

Each area of school has its own set of routines. The moral values or codes of conduct apply everywhere and each person in the school uses a common vocabulary to describe it.

# RESEARCH ON REWARDS AND SANCTIONS

*The following research was completed by the Head of Year at John of Gaunt School, Trowbridge (reproduced with thanks).*

## Questionnaire: Rewards and sanctions

Our emotions are influenced by the rewards and sanctions we receive. Read the following list of preferred rewards of pupils in years 7 to 9, then answer the questions listed below.

| | |
|---|---|
| Letter of praise to parents | Having work on display |
| Rewarded by a commendation | Praised by form tutor |
| Praised by Head of Year | Praised by other pupils |
| Name appearing on a noticeboard | Whole class praised |
| Mentioned in assembly | Non-verbal praise, like a smile |
| Praised by subject teacher | |

**Questions**

1. Number the above points in your order of preference

2. Write out the reward you preferred most, and say why you chose it

Now read the list of sanctions disliked by year 7 and year 9 pupils, then answer the questions listed below.

| | |
|---|---|
| Removed from group | Sent to Year Head/Deputy Head |
| Put on report – parents informed | Removal of privilege |
| Given unpleasant jobs to do | Given lines |
| Told off in front of class/assembly | Told off privately |
| After-school detention | Sent out of class |
| Being kept in at lunchtime | Being moved to another seat |

**Questions**

1. Number the above points in the order you dislike them most

2. Write out the sanction you dislike most and say why this is so

# Results: The importance of rewards

| Reward – nature of praise | Scores (with placing) | | |
|---|---|---|---|
| | **Boys** | **Girls** | **Total** |
| Letter of praise to parents | 624 (1) | 574 (1) | 1198 (1) |
| Reward by commendation | 387 (4) | 384 (4) | 771 (4) |
| Praised by Year Head | 538 (2) | 468 (2) | 1006 (2) |
| Name on noticeboard | 266 (7) | 263 (7) | 529 (7) |
| Mentioned in assembly | 361 (6) | 285 (6) | 646 (6) |
| Praised by subject staff | 406 (3) | 333 (5) | 739 (5) |
| Having work on display | 233 (9) | 232 (8) | 465 (8) |
| Praised by Tutor | 383 (5) | 436 (3) | 819 (3) |
| Praised by other pupils | 245 (8) | 212 (9) | 457 (9) |
| Whole class praised | 230 (10) | 188 (10) | 418 (10) |
| Non-verbal praise, e.g. smile | 117 (11) | 136 (11) | 253 (11) |

# Histogram to show year group's preferred rewards

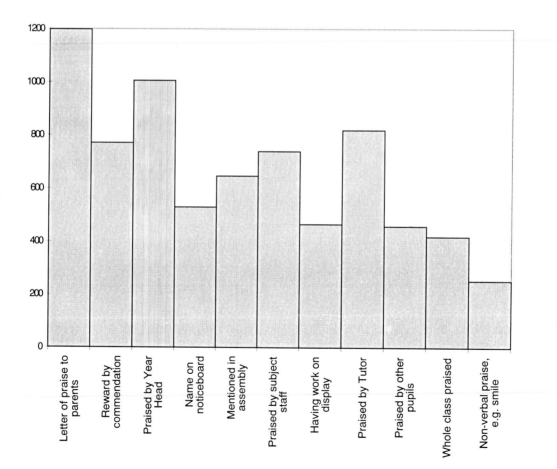

# Results: Pupils' views on sanctions

| Sanction | Scores (with placing) | | |
|---|---|---|---|
| | Boys | Girls | Total |
| Removed from group | 375 (5) | 482 (2) | 857 (5) |
| Put on report – parents informed | 487 (1) | 511 (1) | 998 (1) |
| Given unpleasant jobs to do | 256 (6) | 166 (10) | 422 (8) |
| Told off in front of class | 429 (4) | 479 (3) | 908 (3) |
| After-school detention | 452 (3) | 414 (5) | 866 (4) |
| Lunchtime detention | 239 (7) | 205 (7) | 444 (7) |
| Sent to HOY or Dep. Head | 462 (2) | 470 (4) | 932 (2) |
| Removal of privilege | 194 (9) | 193 (8) | 387 (9) |
| Given lines | 167 (11) | 85 (12) | 252 (12) |
| Told off privately | 176 (10) | 192 (9) | 368 (10) |
| Sent out of class | 205 (8) | 254 (6) | 459 (6) |
| Moved seats | 103 (12) | 151 (11) | 254 (11) |

## Histogram to show year group's most disliked (therefore most effective?) sanctions

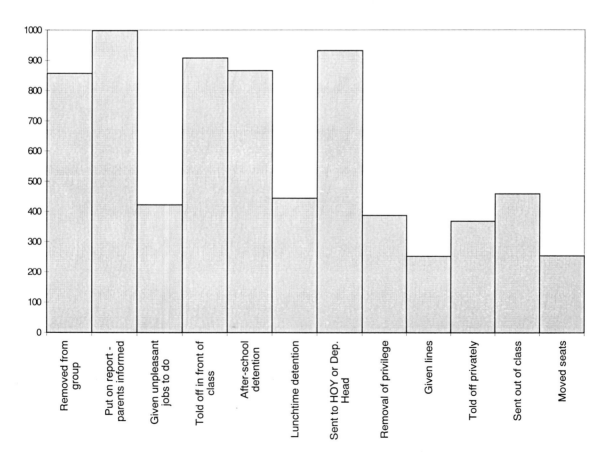

# EXAMPLES OF IDEAS FOR REWARDS

Rewards are divided into '**encouragers**' and '**specials**'.

'Encouragers' are given for abiding by the codes of conduct of the school. There should be a basic entitlement of rewards, including 'encouragers' to reinforce good citizenship.

'Specials' are certificates, positions of responsibility, letters of commendation etc., which can be given for an accumulation of 'encouragers' or for special events.

## A selection of rewards given at the Commonweal School, Swindon

'Encouragers' are housepoints given for good work, good conduct or specific acts of kindness or helpfulness.

After every 10 housepoints, a Certificate of Merit is given in year assemblies.

At 100, 200 and 250 housepoints, Headteacher Awards are given at House Assemblies. These awards are kept in the pupil's Record of Achievement

## Additional Rewards

A variety of additional rewards are available. Past examples have included:

♦ a certificate for attending peer education courses

♦ a certificate for attending a geography field trip

♦ representing the school at a conference

♦ a letter to parents regarding positions of responsibility in the school

# AN IDEA FOR ACKNOWLEDGING GOOD BEHAVIOUR AND DILIGENT WORK

Pupils take the class sheet shown below from one lesson to the next. It is placed on the teacher's desk and s/he only has to make a comment in the 'excellent' or the 'disappointing' columns, the rest are automatically 'good'.

| NAMES | EXCELLENT | GOOD | DISAPPOINTING |
|---|---|---|---|
| Mark Abbott | | | |
| Jane Anster | | | |
| Carl Bather | | | |
| Mary Butterworth | | | |

♦ **Few pupils will be outstanding and require extra comment.**

♦ **Few pupils will ignore the warning and continue with 'disappointing' behaviour and so need comment.**

♦ **The majority will be 'good' (behaving appropriately and 'on-task').**

The list goes to the form tutor at the end of each day and pupils who have not received any 'disappointing' comments are automatically rewarded. Perhaps they could receive a certificate or privilege at the end of each half term.

The 'excellent' can be commended with additional rewards.

The 'disappointing' are highlighted for some kind of sanction.

***THIS SYSTEM IS VERY EASY TO ADMINISTER***

# A CHALLENGE TO SECONDARY SCHOOLS

Lord Elton (1989) wrote:

*'The most effective sanction is the withdrawal of a privilege'*

Is this possible in a secondary school system?

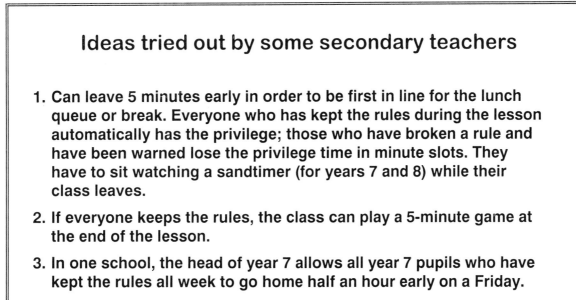

## Ideas tried out by some secondary teachers

1. Can leave 5 minutes early in order to be first in line for the lunch queue or break. Everyone who has kept the rules during the lesson automatically has the privilege; those who have broken a rule and have been warned lose the privilege time in minute slots. They have to sit watching a sandtimer (for years 7 and 8) while their class leaves.

2. If everyone keeps the rules, the class can play a 5-minute game at the end of the lesson.

3. In one school, the head of year 7 allows all year 7 pupils who have kept the rules all week to go home half an hour early on a Friday.

4. In special needs, it is possible to structure privileges much more tightly in order to guarantee success.

# LUNCH
# TIMES

# MUCH OF THE TROUBLE IN SCHOOLS COMES FROM UNSUPERVISED TIME:

◆Fights

◆Bullying

◆Bored behaviours

◆Vandalism

Secondary schools need to address the important issues of a lunchtime policy

# Example: Policy for lunchtime behaviour
# and
# Midday supervision for Years 7-11

*Reproduced with permission from St Lawrence's School Policy, to be displayed in a prominent position in Tutor Rooms*

## 1. Lunch arrangements

Pupils may:

(a)     take cooked meal in Fitzmaurice Refectory
(b)     take packed lunch or snack in Trinity Hall or Drama Studio when Trinity Hall is in use
(c)     go home for lunch

This information will be recorded in register with the following code:

F       Free school meal
H       Home for lunch
M       Hot meal at school
S       Sandwiches

This is important in case of fire drill at lunchtime. No pupil may eat lunch in the Tutor Rooms.

The timing of lunch sittings for year groups will be published in the School Bulletin.

## 2. Use of dining halls

(a)     Pupils are expected to take off coats whilst eating lunch
(b)     Pupils are expected to leave tables clean and tidy
(c)     Good table manners are always expected

## 3. Access to buildings

Pupils may:

(a).     Use only Tutor Room or paired tutor bases as published
(b)     Use Library.
(c)     Use Computer Rooms
(d)     Attend any organised practice or activity

Clearly, with an open school policy, pupils are expected to use buildings and classrooms with care and respect. No pupils should be chasing through buildings or hanging about corridors.

## 4.   Playgrounds

Pupils should not play ball games or run about in areas close to Fitzmaurice or Trinity Buildings.

Home Field is available during the summer for snacks/picnics, as long as all litter is placed in the bins provided.

The following areas are out of bounds:
   Sports field
   Car parks
   End of Home Field and behind Sports Centre at Ashley Road side behind 12th
   Form Area except for access.

## 5. Use of Tutor Rooms

Generally, pupils should be seated and behave in a quiet and sensible way. Pupils can use tutor bases to chat, play board games (chess etc.) or cards, or work quietly. (Gambling of any sort is expressly forbidden and any pupils found playing any card game for reward/money will be severely dealt with). Personal stereos/music machines should not be brought to school unless requested for lessons.

## 6. Quiet study for homework and course work

The Library is the best place for this and will be open from 1pm to 1.50pm. It is hoped that with alterations this area will eventually have 50+ seated places.

## 7. Leaving school premises

All pupils who take lunch on school premises must remain in school at all times.

Year 11 pupils who have written permission of parents have the privilege of leaving the school premises at lunchtime, if they wish. This privilege will be withdrawn if abused.

Year 11 pupils should of course sign in and out in the usual way at reception.

## 8. Misbehaviour

In the first instance, Midday Supervisory staff will warn pupils or refer to the Senior Staff Supervisor on duty that day.

In cases of serious misconduct, the Senior Supervisor will refer pupils to the Headteacher.

Pupils referred to the Head or duty management team member will:

(a)      Have name and behaviour recorded
(b)      Have details circulated to Year Head and Tutor.

If a pupil is referred to the Head more than once in a half term, then parents will be asked to take over their supervision at home, for the duration of the lunch break.

Where groups of pupils misbehave in Tutor Rooms, they will be managed through the referral procedure and not by the closure of the Tutor Room.

Clearly, any member of staff, teaching or non-teaching, who notices dangerous or unacceptable behaviour, should take appropriate action. Often a warning is sufficient; and then passing on the pupil's name to the Year Head or Tutor helps to reinforce to pupils that we are all concerned to have a calm and safe environment.

# PRIMARY SCHOOLS OFFER:

♦ **Supervised dining hall**

♦ **Playground Friends**

♦ **Friendship Stops**

♦ **Zoned areas of the playground for different activities**

♦ **Equipment for play**

♦ **A quiet area to avoid the boisterous games**

♦ **A football policy with equal opportunities**

♦ **Consistent rules that apply inside and outside of the school building**

*What are secondary schools doing to make lunch times emotionally and physically safe for all pupils, so that afternoon learning is not sabotaged by events of the lunch hour?*

# CHILDREN 'BEYOND'

Children 'beyond' are those whose behaviour is extremely challenging. It is helpful to see these pupils as exhibiting behaviour that is consistent with their world view. The behaviour we as teachers find so difficult serves the purpose of keeping the pupil's inner world 'safe'. That means safe from relationships that might require him/her to change.

## Children 'beyond' are trapped in a negative and cumulative cycle of poor self-esteem

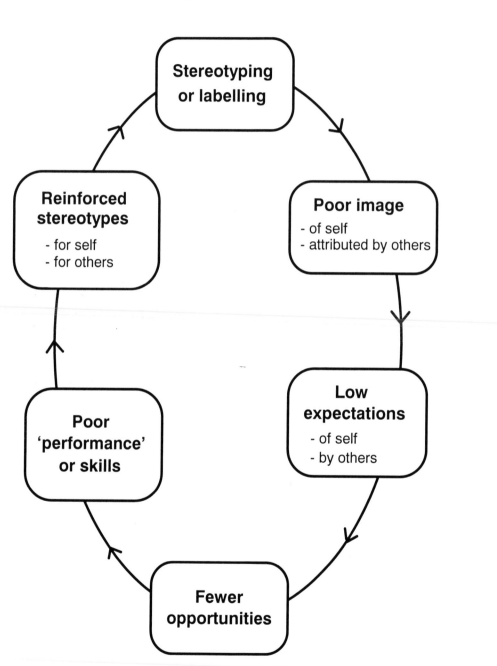

**For the child 'beyond', we must provide opportunities to disregard any previous negative labelling**

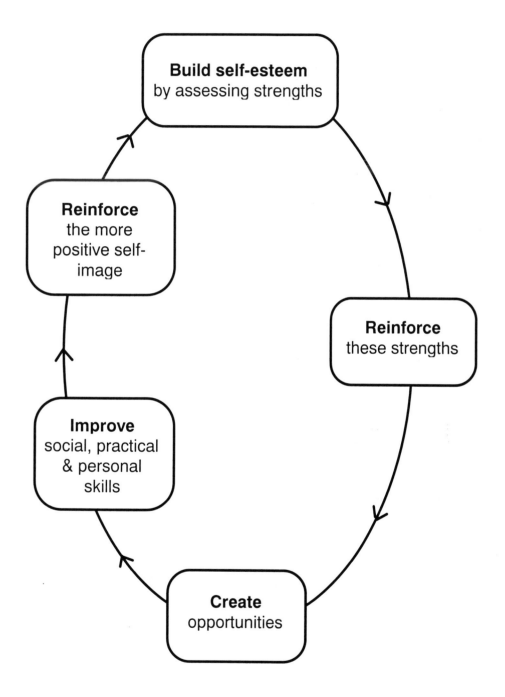

# IDENTIFYING CHILDREN 'BEYOND'

**One way of identifying children 'beyond' is to ask staff to fill in the following inventory of behaviours for young people at risk of disaffection.**

| |
|---|
| Do you have any pupil in your Year 7 or 8 teaching group that regularly causes you some concern? If so, please put the pupil's name in the box and then tick the behaviours that are most often shown by this pupil. <br><br> Many thanks. We hope this will help us to choose the right pupils to join a proposed support group. |
| **Name of pupil** |
| **Name of teacher** |

| A. Behaviour characterised by lack of self control | |
|---|---|
| 1. Often arrives late with excuses about forgetting which lesson it was, or having returned to previous lesson to find some lost possessions. | |
| 2. During lessons calls out loudly and repeatedly. Often puts up hand without knowing the answer – or even remembering the question. | |
| 3. Rarely has the appropriate equipment. | |
| 4. Cannot concentrate when given verbal or written instructions – will ask questions immediately. | |
| 5. After a short attempt at task becomes very restless and fidgety. | |
| 6. When questioned about that task has forgotten its initial purpose. | |
| 7. Is unable to work independently or make balanced decisions at any time. | |
| 8. Is physically clumsy. | |
| 9. Actively distracts others from their work. | |

| B. Withdrawn behaviour | |
|---|---|
| 1. Will sit alone or else has to be 'put beside' partner. | |
| 2. Never volunteers information, puts up hand or asks for clarification. | |
| 3. If directly questioned, looks embarrassed, may blush or fidget. | |

| | |
|---|---|
| 4. Rarely smiles. | |
| 5. Will often be the focus of other pupils' derisory or uncomplimentary comments. | |
| 6. Body posture is often stooped or awkward in movement. | |
| 7. Is seen to be isolated in playground or walking around the school. | |
| 8. Is occasionally absent from sessions. | |
| 9. Often eyes are downcast. Is unable to sustain eye-contact with others. | |

| **C. Hostile behaviour** | |
|---|---|
| 1. Rarely shows interest in content of lesson or its related discussions. | |
| 2. When questioned, will either look away from teacher in bored or calculated insolence – or else will stare directly with a challenging aggressive stance. | |
| 3. Will always sit away or turn back towards you if given the opportunity. | |
| 4. Will never initiate a conversation with an adult unless it is related to the pupil's feeling of having been unfairly treated, pupil's boredom or any other topic that elicits his/her contempt. | |
| 5. Deliberately attempts to stop lesson's progress, or conversely will express alienation by complete lack of attention, arriving very late or not at all. | |
| 6. Occasional bursts of aggressive behaviour, either towards the teacher or towards peers. | |
| 7. Deliberate destruction or vandalism of school property. | |
| 8. Actively distracts others in a deliberate attempt to disrupt lesson. | |

# EXAMPLES OF GOOD PRACTICE WITH CHILDREN 'BEYOND'

## The use of peer support groups

**Peer support in High Schools: a programme to complement pastoral care strategies**, Graham Bourgault, *Pastoral Care in Education*, June 1991

Graham Bourgault outlines a successful way of providing opportunities and support to two separate groups of Australian high school students. Those in the new intake year have the support of individual older students who thus enable them to settle in to a new environment more easily; the older pupils gain the training and experience of the peer support programme, which becomes an important part of their own personal development

**Approaches to peer support: befriending, counselling and mediation**, Helen Cowie, *Young Minds Newsletter*, Issue 23, October 1985

This article outlines approaches to peer support.

**'A little help from my friends': a secondary school peer support programme**, Peter Kaye & Alastair Webb, *Pastoral Care in Education*, June 1996

Perth High School ran an experimental programme developed from the approach generally described as peer support. In this case the programme was developed from an Australian personal and social education scheme. Like the schools in Australia, Perth High School was partly concerned to ease the transition from primary school to secondary school.

**Orchestrating success in personal, social and educational areas: using peer support**, Tony Charlton & Kenneth David, *Pastoral Care in Education*, March 1997

Charlton and David argue that counselling is not the only form of support available to pupils – and they in fact suggest that 'counselling' may be an overused term. They highlight pupils' need and right to be listened to. They go on to point out that in busy classrooms, teachers may not always find time to listen to and adequately support pupils. Alternative 'listening' facilities via peer support are discussed. Finally, the benefits of this peer resource are outlined for teachers as well as those administering and in receipt of help.

## Small-scale therapeutic circles

**An evaluative account of the working of a dramatherapy peer support group within a comprehensive school**, Jenny Mosley, *Support for Learning*, vol.6 no.4, 1991

This article outlines the use of dramatherapy with pupils experiencing behavioural difficulty. Jenny Mosley has carefully researched the topic and evolved a strategy for structuring therapeutic sessions that will help such pupils. She clearly describes and justifies this strategy.

**Providing emotional support through circle-time: a case study**, Mollie Curry, *Support for Learning*, vol.12 no.3, 1997

The East Devon Behaviour Support Team uses circle time as a mutually supportive system. The case study provides a fascinating insight into how the behaviour of a child, previously isolated, changed to such a degree that she became a valued and accepted member of the class.

**Developing peer support groups**, Kath Shaw, *Pastoral Care in Education*, October 1991

This is a practical INSET response to the Elton Report. It describes work initiated in her school.

# Circles can be used to write IEPs

**Margaret Goldthorpe's book *Effective IEPs through Circle Time* outlines how circles and peer support can be used to support pupils with emotional and behavioural needs 'beyond' the normal range of strategies outlined in the Whole School Quality Circle Time Model.**

The book contains case studies of ways in which circle time is used to create a team spirit and valuing ethos to support peers.

Chapters of particular relevance cover:

- ♦ **Writing the IEP**
- ♦ **Aims and targets**
- ♦ **Strategies**
- ♦ **Incentives as strategies**
- ♦ **Sharing the IEP**
- ♦ **Desperate cases – desperate measures**
- ♦ **Special needs circle times.**

# LOOKING AFTER YOURSELF – TEACHER ENERGY LEVELS

# *OUR* SELF-ESTEEM IS ALSO VERY IMPORTANT

*Jot down the answers to these questions on your own. Be as honest with yourself as possible.*

## What I like about myself

In answer to the following questions, think of one thing in each category that has made you feel good about yourself.

| | |
|---|---|
| 1. Anything I have done in my job | |
| 2. Any skill I have | |
| 3. Anything I have achieved that took a great deal of effort | |
| 4. Any spare time activities | |
| 5. Anything I do that helps others | |
| 6. Any feature of my personality | |
| 7. Any way in which I have changed | |
| 8. Any fears I have overcome | |
| 9. Anything I have thought, said, written or done | |
| 10. Any way in which I relate to others | |

**List the three most important things you do or have that have added to your self-confidence.**

**List the three things you would like to feel more confident about.**

# HOW TO IMPROVE SELF-ESTEEM IN YOUR PROFESSIONAL LIFE

*Low self-esteem has a profound effect on our lives. It affects the way we view our own ability to respond to certain 'trigger' events or situations. Low self-esteem therefore traps us in a negative cycle of failure, which creates a self-fulfilling prophecy and prevents us from ever leaving the cycle to enjoy any positive progress. The theoretical models of positive and negative cycles show how practical exercises of thinking and challenging 'old' negative beliefs can enhance self-esteem and subsequently improve the quality of your professional life.*

# The treadmill of low self-esteem

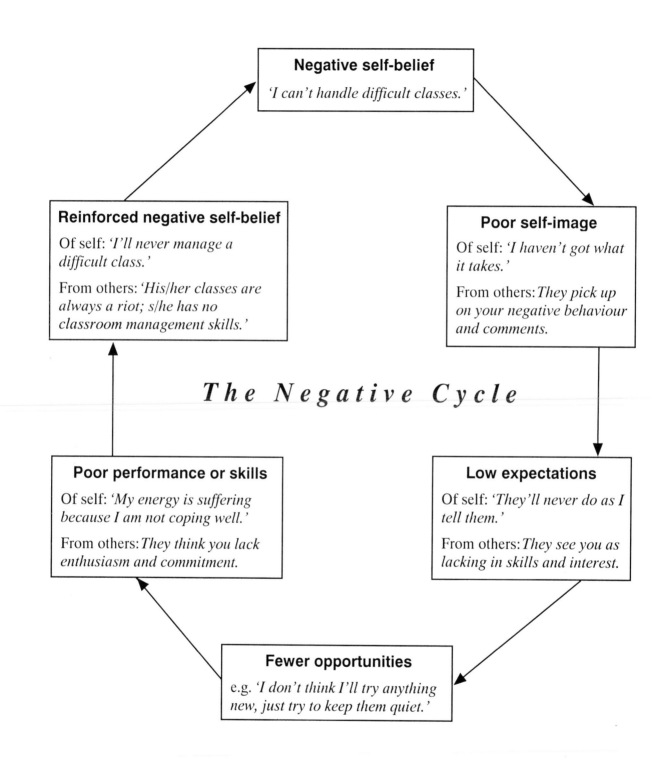

**Negative self-belief**

*'I can't handle difficult classes.'*

**Reinforced negative self-belief**

Of self: *'I'll never manage a difficult class.'*

From others: *'His/her classes are always a riot; s/he has no classroom management skills.'*

**Poor self-image**

Of self: *'I haven't got what it takes.'*

From others: *They pick up on your negative behaviour and comments.*

*The Negative Cycle*

**Poor performance or skills**

Of self: *'My energy is suffering because I am not coping well.'*

From others: *They think you lack enthusiasm and commitment.*

**Low expectations**

Of self: *'They'll never do as I tell them.'*

From others: *They see you as lacking in skills and interest.*

**Fewer opportunities**

e.g. *'I don't think I'll try anything new, just try to keep them quiet.'*

# The upward cycle of good self-esteem

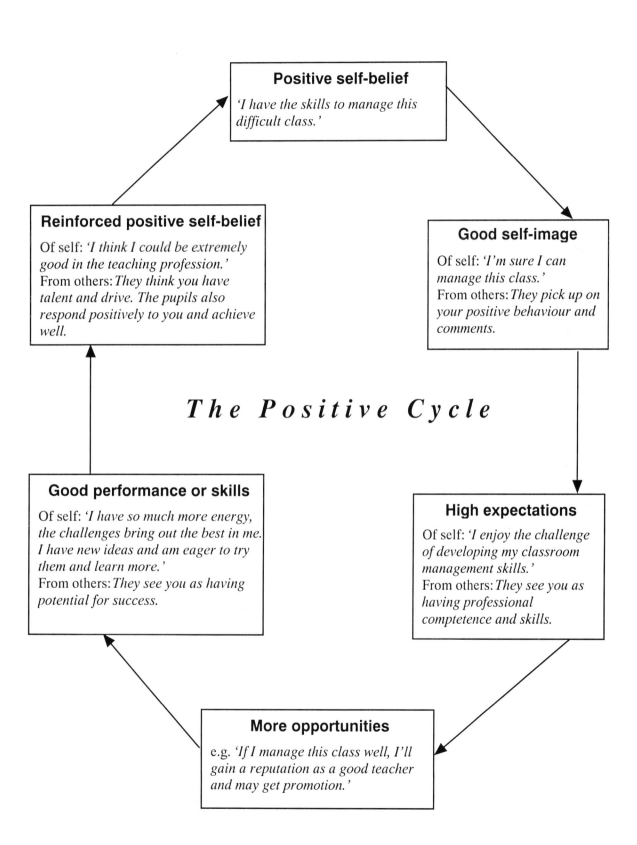

**Positive self-belief**

*'I have the skills to manage this difficult class.'*

**Good self-image**

Of self: *'I'm sure I can manage this class.'*
From others: *They pick up on your positive behaviour and comments.*

**Reinforced positive self-belief**

Of self: *'I think I could be extremely good in the teaching profession.'*
From others: *They think you have talent and drive. The pupils also respond positively to you and achieve well.*

*The Positive Cycle*

**High expectations**

Of self: *'I enjoy the challenge of developing my classroom management skills.'*
From others: *They see you as having professional comptetence and skills.*

**Good performance or skills**

Of self: *'I have so much more energy, the challenges bring out the best in me. I have new ideas and am eager to try them and learn more.'*
From others: *They see you as having potential for success.*

**More opportunities**

e.g. *'If I manage this class well, I'll gain a reputation as a good teacher and may get promotion.'*

# Develop a personal care plan in order to create energy and restore balance

Make sure you 'drink' from each of these five wells at least once every week. Spend time on yourself to keep mentally healthy and well balanced; able to keep the job in perspective.

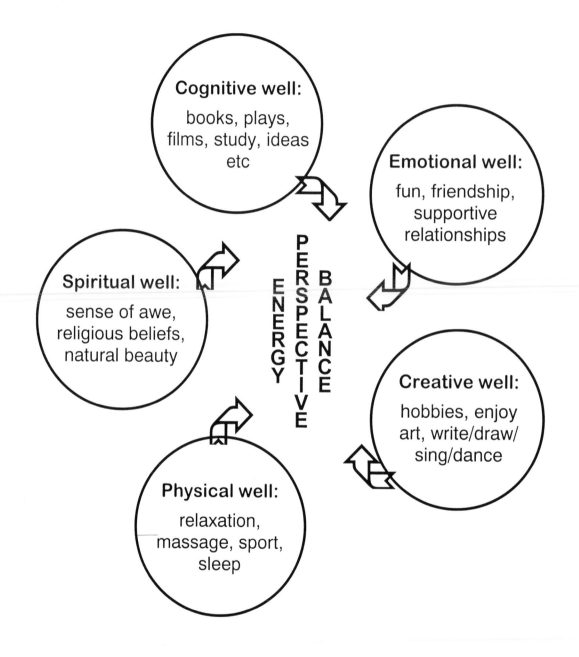

# ADULT CIRCLE TIME

All adults in the school ideally need their own circles where issues are discussed.

In the Quality Circle Time Model, circle meetings would be available on a regular basis for all the following groups of people:

| | |
|---|---|
| **PUPILS** | Once a week or once a fortnight, depending on timetable and pressure of administration |
| **SCHOOL COUNCIL** | Whole school issues taken to school council circle once a half term |
| **TEACHING STAFF** | In departments, once a half term<br>As a whole staff, once a term |
| **SUPPORT STAFF** | Once a half term |
| **OFFICE STAFF** | Once a half term |
| **MIDDAY SUPERVISORS** | Once a half term |
| **MAINTENANCE STAFF** | Once a half term |

# Ground rules for adult circle meetings

◆ Try and take a genuine interest by listening well to whoever is speaking

◆ Respect people's right to an opinion; even though you may not believe their opinion is right

◆ Remember, if you disagree with someone, you also have the right to challenge them; but only respectfully

◆ Avoid making judgements about people: remember there are many different 'facets' to people, you may only be seeing one side of them

◆ Take responsibility for your own decision to contribute or not contribute

◆ Stay calm and non-defensive

◆ Disentangle the issue from the person

◆ Use 'I' and speak for yourself

◆ When possible, genuinely thank people for their contribution

◆ Be sensitive to other people's individual styles of communication

◆ Show integrity by not talking about people's issues outside the circle meeting

◆ Be prepared to apologise sometimes

◆ Keep your sense of humour.

◆ Forgive often; it's not worth losing precious energy by 'festering' about people

◆ Keep your sense of humour and perspective

# SUMMARY

## with

### bibliography,

### user comments,

### training opportunities

### & resources

## My energy

- Build in Golden Moments
- Set your boundaries
- Take a lunchbreak
- Visit 'wells' and set your TATTs*
- Develop your Personal Care Plan
- Be kind to yourself
- Help others with these ideas

## Looking after the team

- Staff Social Committee -- have fun, encourage, but do not force
- End meetings on a positive note
- Have your own circle times to help each other
- Celebrate success and achievement
- Value each others' strengths and work on your needs

## Quality Circle Time Model

- Timetable once a week
- Remember structure: starting game, round, open forum, celebrate success, closing ritual
- Make it fun
- View and further your own skills and qualities
- Use suggestion box for ideas for circle
- Remind pupils that if they say anything that worries you, you may have to take it further

## Golden Rules

- Keep Golden Rules separate from safety routines
- Display in every classroom and public areas
- Constantly remind and refer to them
- Teach these moral codes in circle time
- Become a role model of Golden Rules
- Relate incentives directly to Golden Rules
- Copy and send to parents for signature and agreement

## Incentives

- Make them appropriate; negotiate them with pupils
- Individual and whole class reward systems
- Devise encouragers and specials
- Ensure every adult and pupil has access to incentives

## Sanctions

- Be careful your own sanctions have not become incentives
- Make sure they are consistently applied
- Warning system is essential: visual warning cards
- Best sanction is the withdrawal of a privilege

\* Tiny Achievable Tickable Targets

## Lunchtime policy

◆ Raise status of supervisors
◆ Find ways of valuing supervisors
◆ Divide playground into activity areas
◆ Develop safe and equal opportunities football
◆ Develop teacher/supervisor communication systems that link lunchtime supervisors into the school system
◆ If possible hold two half-hour circle time meetings for supervisors per half term
◆ Devise positions of responsibility for pupils

## Children 'beyond'

◆ Check all earlier stages have been used and that motivation strategies were appropriate
◆ Use TATTs
◆ Whole class support given to child's TATTs system
◆ Therapeutic support – i.e. small circle
◆ Investigate the possibility that Circle Time can be used to support IEP

## Containment and review

◆ Staff team support: the pupil at Stage 4 is not one teacher's responsibility
◆ Urgent help needed? Have prior reciprocal arrangement with colleagues re: Red Alert!
◆ Recognise that success is not always possible; mental health and sanity of staff and rest of the class are paramount

# BIBLIOGRAPHY

**Jenny Mosley's books are listed in the Training and Resources section on page 79.**

Baldwin, J. & Wells, H., *Active Tutorial Work*. London, Blackwell, 1980

Benson, J., *Working More Creatively with Groups*. Routledge, 1987

Beynon, J., *Initial Encounters in the Secondary School*. London, Falmer Press, 1985

Bliss, T. & Tetley, J., *Circle Time. For infant, junior and secondary schools*. Lucky Duck Publishing

Bourgault, G., 'Peer support in High Schools: a programme to complement pastoral care strategies', *Pastoral Care in Education*, June 1991

Brandes, D., *Gamester's Two*. Hutchinson 1982

Brandes, D. & Ginnis, P., *A Guide to Student Centred Learning*. Oxford, Blackwell, 1986

Brandes, D. & Ginnis, P., *Student Centred Schools*. Oxford, Blackwell, 1991

Brandes, D. & Phillips, H., *Gamester's Handbook*. Hutchinson, 1978

Burns, R., *The Self Concept*. London, Longman, 1979

Burns, R., *Self-Concept Development and Education*. Eastbourne, Holt Rinehart and Winston, 1982

Button, L., *Group Tutoring for the Form Teacher: Lower School* and *Upper School*. Hodder & Stoughton, 1981 and 1982

Chamberlain, R., 'Ground Rules: a case for their use in the classroom', *Pastoral Care in Education*, pp.26-30, December 1992

Charlton, T. & David, K., 'Orchestrating success in personal, social and educational areas: using peer support', *Pastoral Care in Education*, pp.24-28, March 1997

Cowie, H., 'Approaches to peer support: befriending, counselling and mediation', *Young Minds Newsletter*, no.23, October 1985

Cowie, H. & Sharp, S., 'Students tackle the problem of bullying', *Pastoral Care in Education*, pp.31-37, 1992

Curry, M., 'Providing emotional support through circle-time: a case study', *Support for Learning*, vol.12 no.3, 1997

Douglas, T., *Groups: Understanding people gathered together*. London, Tavistock, 1983

Douglas, T., *Basic Groupwork*. London, Tavistock/Routledge, 1986

Douglas, T., *The Handbook of Common Groupwork Problems*. London, Tavistock/Routledge, 1991

Elton, Lord (Chairman), *Discipline in Schools: Report of the Committee of Enquiry*. London, HMSO 1989

Egan, G., *The Skilled Helper: a problem management approach to helping*. Brooks Cole, 1975

Gardner, H., *The Unschooled Mind: how children think and how schools should teach.* London, Fontana, 1991

Gardner, H., *Multiple Intelligences: the theory in practice.* London, Basic Books, 1993

Glasser, W., *Schools Without Failure.* New York, Harper Crompton Books, 1969

Goleman, D., *Emotional Intelligence: Why it matters more than IQ.* London, Bloomsbury, 1996

Gordon, T., *Teacher Effectiveness Training.* New York, David McKay, 1974

Greenhalgh, P., *Emotional Growth and Learning.* London, Routledge, 1994

Hall, E. & Hall, C., *Human Relationships in Education.* Routledge, 1989

Hopson, B. & Scally, M., *Lifeskills Teaching.* London, McGraw Hill, 1981

Jacobs, M., Turk, B. & Horn, E., *Building Positive Self-Concept: 113 activities for adolescents.* Portland, Maine, J. Weston Walch, 1988

Kaye, P. & Webb, A., 'A little help from my friends: a secondary school peer support programme, *Pastoral Care in Education,* June 1996

LaBenne, W. D. & Green, A. I., *Educational Implications of Self-Concept Theory.* Pacific Palisades, Goodyear, 1969

Lawrence, D., *Enhancing Self-Esteem in the Classroom.* London, Paul Chapman, 1988

Maslow, A., *Towards a Psychology of Being.* New York, Van Nostrand Reinhold, 1962

Mosley, J., 'Some implications arising from a small-scale study of a circle-based programme initiated for the tutorial period', *Pastoral Care in Education,* vol.6 no.2, pp. 10-17, June 1988

Mosley, J., 'An evaluative account of the working of a dramatherapy peer support group within a comprehensive school', *Support for Learning,* vol.6 no.4, pp.156-164, 1991

Mosley, J., *What is circle time?* 1992

Mosley, J., 'Is there a place for counselling in schools?', *Journal for the British Association of Counselling,* vol.4 no.2, May 1993

Nelson-Jones, R., *The theory and practice of counselling psychology.* London, Cassell, 1982

Nelson-Jones, R., *Human Relationship: a skills approach.* Holt Rinehart and Winston, 1989

Purkey, W.W., *Self Concept and School Achievement.* Englewood Cliffe NJ, Prentice Hall, 1970

Rogers, C., *Freedom to Learn for the 80s.* Merril, USA, Macmillan, 1983

Sharp, S., Sellars, A. & Cowie, H., 'Time to listen: setting up a peer counselling service to help tackle the problem of bullying in schools', *Pastoral Care in Education,* 1994, pp.3-6

Shaw, K., 'Developing Peer Support Groups: a practical INSET response to the Elton Report', *Pastoral Care in Education,* October 1991.

# JENNY MOSLEY CONSULTANCIES

Jenny Mosley Consultancies has run many successful INSET days for secondary schools (see page 78 for details). Written reports and evaluations of courses testify to our expertise in enabling teachers to develop their range of personal and professional skills.

*'I would like to take this opportunity to thank you for the splendid day you provided As you will no doubt have gathered from the conference evaluation, your contribution was highly valued by all of our members: "fascinating", "excellent", "the quality of presentation was first class" and lastly "this was one of the most thought-provoking days I have experienced in a long while." These comments speak for themselves.'*

**Chairman of Deputy Heads Association**

*'For the school as a whole it did much to boost the feeling of trust and confidence in the Appraisal system and has helped considerably in creating the right climate.'*

**Deputy Head**

*'I now recognise the importance of the peer support model in my own development and that of my colleagues. I feel strongly that INSET is a vastly underrated instrument of change. When used creatively in this way, it can be a potent vehicle for changing teachers' attitudes. The evidence would suggest that staff are more open to change when they observe outside consultants working "on the shop floor" with the children.'*

**Head of Special Needs Department**

*'The day was a roaring success and has lightened my task considerably.'*

**Headteacher**

*'On behalf of the school and particularly the SD Committee, I am writing to thank you for the most successful INSET day in living memory. As you will see from the evaluations – so many people found the day stimulating and thought-provoking.'*

**INSET Organiser**
**Deputy Head**

# Children speak

*'I feel this Circle Time is a great idea ... If we had time to just talk and let go of all the things we were holding inside us, without someone breathing down our necks and trying to shut us up. It would first calm us down and second we could think better. I wish we had something like this here, I have so many things to say.'*

**Rishabh Shah, 13 years**

*'I liked passing the egg around and voicing our opinions. I thought it was cool how people had different opinions about different things.'*

**Sarah, 12 years.**

*'This will help the student-teacher relationship in our lives become stronger and closer ... this 30-minute period can have an effect on our entire lives.'*

**Nizia Vasi, 14 years**

*'I would like to discuss why I am left out of almost everything. Also I would ask my teacher why girls are regarded as "dirty" to boys and why boys are regarded as "dirty" to girls.'*

**Richa Bakshi, 11 years**

*'I think it did help to build friendships because you learn that a lot of people share the same views as you, so you find new friends.'*

**Sasha, 11 years**

*'The other people in the class might have had the same problem they could help the person solve the problem. And we could do it in the form of a game so it becomes much more fun for us.'*

**Akshina Samtani, 12 years**

*'The circle helped everyone to take part. In my old school when we did PSE we used to sit in rows in desks and in the circle we could see everybody and it was much easier to talk.'*

**Lucy, 12 years**

# TRAINING AND RESOURCES

## Training for your staff

The Jenny Mosley Consultancies can provide well-trained consultants, experienced in all aspects of the Whole School Quality Circle Time Model, who will visit your school to run courses and workshops for teachers and support staff. Try our key introductory course for primary and secondary schools on the **Whole School Quality Circle Time Model**:

♦ On a Closure (INSET) day, all staff, teachers, lunchtime supervisors, ancillary and administration staff are invited to participate in a day that focuses on all aspects of the model, including team-building, developing positive ethos and valuing individuals.

♦ On a Working In School day, the school does not close and the Quality Circle Time approach is demonstrated with whole groups of pupils observed by a range of staff. In addition, Circle Time meetings can be held for lunchtime supervisors and an action plan for the school is drawn up with key members of staff.

♦ The Top Value Option (discounted price) is to book both the above plus a follow-up day for evaluation and advice.

## Some of the other courses we offer

**Happier Lunchtimes**

**Assessing the Effectiveness of Self-Esteem, Anti-bullying and Positive Behaviour Policies**

**Developing Peer Mediation**

**Developing PSHE, Citizenship and Emotional Literacy Policies through Quality Circle Time**

**Re-energising your Circle Time Policies with Quality Ideas**

**Children Beyond – What more can we do?**

**Involving Everyone in Quality Circle Time**

Quality Circle Time mentoring is also available, as are courses in staff development and support covering areas such as team-building, stress management, developing your own self-esteem, boosting your energy and basic counselling skills.

---

### Accredited, specialist trainers only!

Our research and experience reveal that the Whole School Quality Circle Time Model can become diluted or vulnerable when people who have never attended one of our in-depth courses offer training based on our model. Each year Jenny Mosley holds week long in-depth courses nationally and then awards accompanying certificates, renewable annually.

---

**For details and to discuss possibilities, contact our Project Manager.**

# Books and other resources

**Quality Circle Time in the Primary Classroom** by Jenny Mosley
Essential guide to enhancing self-esteem and self-discipline, for teachers wishing to put the Whole School Circle Time model into their classrooms, with hundreds of ideas and lesson plans. (LDA)

**Quality Circle Time in the Secondary School** by Jenny Mosley & Marilyn Tew
Explains the Quality Circle Time Model and its application with older pupils. Supporting teachers to enhance their own self-empowerment and to inspire it in others, the book offers over 100 themed activities and practical strategies to enhance behaviour management and anti-bullying policies. Useful examples prove it's never too late to introduce Quality Circle Time. (David Fulton)

**Bridging the Circle: Transition through Quality Circle Time** by Anne Cowling & Penny Vine
Featuring lesson plans for years 6 and 7, with effective and invaluable strategies to support the often intimidating transition from primary to secondary school. Includes photocopiable resources and ideas for encouraging parental understanding and support. (Positive Press)

**Effective IEPs through Circle Time** by Margaret Goldthorpe
Practical solutions to writing Individual Education Plans for children with emotional and behavioural difficulties, using Quality Circle Time. (LDA)

**Personal Power: How to fulfil your private and professional life** by Jenny Mosley & Eileen Gillibrand
An A4 self-help workbook written to complement the authors' counselling and career development programmes for women (although equally valuable to both sexes). Packed with self-assessment exercises about self-esteem, assertiveness, handling stress, time management and more. (Positive Press)

**She Who Dares Wins: A woman's guide to professional and personal success** by Jenny Mosley & Eileen Gillibrand
A developed and extended version of *Personal Power*, this book helps clarify decisions about what you need or want, how you might get there and what might help or hinder your progress. With stepping stones for building self-esteem and strategies for challenging negative thinking 'blocks', an excellent book for assessing whether you are supporting or thwarting the success you deserve. (Positive Press)

**Boost Your Energy: For women juggling home and work** by Eileen Gillibrand & Jenny Mosley
Published originally as *When I Go to Work I Feel Guilty*, here is an in-depth self-help book for working mothers, enabling you to examine the balance in your life and recognise areas needing attention in the interests of boosting and sustaining your energy. Looking at your relationship with yourself, your child and your work, every page offers food for thought and inspiration. (Positive Press)

We also have many books on Quality Circle Time for the Foundation Stage and Primary Schools, and the following new titles in preparation:

*Golden Moments for Busy Teachers*
*The Magic Touch – Tips for Terrific Teachers and Trainers*

**Golden Moment Mug**

Eye-catching blue and gold mug to help you recharge your energy in that precious break from the demands of teaching.

Our catalogue contains many resources for Primary School use, some of which can find a place in Quality Circle Time sessions for secondary schools. Why not buy one of our amazing and relaxing **Rainsticks**, made in South America from a hollow giant cactus spine and producing wonderful watery sounds as grains trickle down inside. Use as a talking object, sound effects for stories or as a shaken percussion instrument.

---

*For further details and to order contact:*

**Jenny Mosley Consultancies / Positive Press Ltd**

*Training*: **Tel. 01225 767157  Fax 01225 755631**

*Books and products*: **Tel. 01225 719204  Fax 01225 712187**

**E-mail circletime@jennymosley.demon.co.uk**

**28A Gloucester Road, Trowbridge,**

**Wiltshire, BA14 0AA**

**Website www.jennymosley.demon.co.uk**